PURPOSEFUL LIVING

Wisdom for Coming of Age in Complex Times

Art Blanchford

Other Resources by Art Blanchford

The 8 Steps to Mastering Mid-Life Transition, available on www.artblanchford.com

Life in Transition Podcast, available on www.lifeintransitionpodcast.com and wherever you listen to podcasts.

Friday Reflections weekly blog on growth and life's learnings, available on www.artblanchford.com/blog

DEDICATIONS

This book is dedicated to my children—Alex, Sawyer, and Kayli—who make my life so much deeper, richer, and more meaningful and help me grow to levels I never would have approached without them. Thank you for your love, challenges, play, trust, and connection, and most of all for showing me what is important in life: You and how to love unconditionally. I would never have learned that without you. I am proud of each of you and love you all "to the moon and back."

All my heart,

Dad

*****

It is also dedicated to my wife, life partner, and best friend, Tonya. My life, especially our wonderful family, is not possible without you. Thank you for showing me the meaning of being worthy in a way I had never experienced. Thank you for loving me through all the craziness, helping me go for my dreams, and making our lives so much more fun and meaningful. I am deeply grateful.

I love you with all that I am,

Art

My family about the time I started writing this book.

And about when I finished writing it.

TABLE OF CONTENTS

INTRODUCTION

Thank you for taking the time to read this book. I am finishing this introduction on my back deck in Brentwood, TN, in January 2024, and much has happened since I wrote most of this book in 2014 and 2015, but that is the subject of another book. I am now a semi-retired, global automotive business executive, a husband of almost 30 years, and a very proud and engaged father of three: two boys and a girl, Alex, Sawyer, and Kayli. Alex and Kayli are adopted from Russia and China, respectively. When I began writing this book, my children were 14, 11, and 9 years old. I'm also an avid adventurer, Ironman triathlete, backpacker, ultra-marathoner, and curious growth seeker. Much of my life has been shaped by anxiety and a deep need to please others – a response to the trauma of growing up in a religious cult. I also have five siblings and four cousins I was raised with and am still super close to today. I struggled tremendously coming of age. And the world is much more complex now. So, I wrote this book primarily for my children, to pass along some of the lessons that I have learned through all the suffering and growth I have experienced on the path to creating what I thought was a very successful life. Some of the points are written directly to them, as it was initially written for them. Please accept that. I highly value personal growth, and I saw my kids struggling with many of the same issues I had. I wanted to share my lessons with them so that they could move on to higher-quality struggles sooner in life than I had. In the eight to ten years between starting to write this and getting it published, my kids have not read this book, but I have lived these lessons myself and have actively engaged with my children, teaching them these lessons personally. This is especially so in the last three years, when I stepped back from my executive role in a large public company and started an ongoing spiritual transformation through a 12-step recovery, where seeking and doing God's will is at the center of everything I do.

This book is for you if you are trying to learn the lessons that will lead to a richer, more meaningful life, with higher-quality struggles, and more joy and satisfaction for you and/or the children you are raising. I'm very grateful to you, the reader, because you are the one who has inspired me to finally finish this book and helped to refine my own thinking and connect more deeply with my own children. The book is arranged to flow from the foundational lessons to the more specific ones. That being said, you can pick it up and read any chapter and take away that specific lesson or tool. Reading this book, I hope that you will garner deeper understandings and new tools that will allow you and those that you love to live more connected, loving, belonging, fulfilling, adventurous, richer, and meaningful lives. Thank you and may God bless you!

Art Blanchford
(Brentwood, Tennessee)

PART 1: FINDING YOUR VOICE

Chapter 1:
You Are Worthy!

"When you get to a place where you understand that love and belonging, your worthiness, is a birthright and not something you have to earn, anything is possible."

~ Brené Brown

This is the single most important thing you can ever understand. Let me say that again, since it is so true and so critical. You are worthy, and that is the single most important thing for you to know in your life. God doesn't make any junk. God doesn't make mistakes. You are perfectly you, just the way you are. And just being you makes you worthy of all the good life has to offer. That's it! You don't have to look a certain way. You don't have to behave a certain way. You don't have to earn it. You don't have to be rich. You don't have to be fit. You don't have to be happy. You don't have to do or be anything. YOU ARE WORTHY! Just by being you, you are worthy of love, joy, peace, happiness, and courage. You don't have to earn it. It is your birthright. As it says in the Bible, you are a child of God, and He is in you, and you are in Him. Let that sink in. You are in God, and God is in you. You are a part of God. You can't be more worthy than that. Marianne Williamson says it best in her wonderful book, *A Return to Love.*

"Our deepest fear is not that we are inadequate. Our deepest fear is that we are powerful beyond measure. It is our light, not our darkness, that most frightens us. We ask ourselves, 'Who am I to be brilliant, gorgeous, talented, fabulous?' Actually, who are you not to be? You are a child of God. You playing small does not serve the world. There is nothing enlightened about shrinking so that other people won't feel insecure around you. We are all meant to shine, as children do. We were born to make manifest the glory of God that is within us. It's not just in some of us; it's in everyone. And as we let our own light shine, we unconsciously give other people permission to do the same. As we are liberated from our own fear, our presence automatically liberates others."

Like everyone else, I am sure you suffer from times of doubt when you feel you are not worthy. You feel you are not good enough, or something enough, to be loved, honored, adored, cherished, and loved some more, to the moon and back. Lord knows I did, and for a *long* time. I have struggled with this my whole life, up until I was 40 years old, and even a little after that. I was plagued by self-doubt and the feeling that I was not good enough to be loved just the way I was. Since I wasn't inherently good enough, I had to do good and achieve things to EARN love. That is part of the reason I did so well in school and helped so much around the home growing up. I felt I had to earn love, acceptance, appreciation, and belonging by doing good things. In school, I studied hard and paid attention so that the teachers would like me. (And any time I say 'like,' it means love, but that just sounds a little weird.) I grew up in a religious cult and homestead, where my parents were more focused on spiritual work than on their 6 kids and our two cousins in the home. Therefore, I did many chores: milked cows before school, chopped wood, started the fires to heat water and cook, tended the fields, cleaned the house, butchered animals, and cooked and did laundry so we would stay warm and fed, and so my parents would love me. When I started working at 6 years old, I worked hard so my lawn-mowing clients would like me. When I started my career, I doubled the intensity, stressed out a lot, and pushed myself beyond the breaking point so that my bosses and customers would like me. I earned a lot of money and gave my wife a great lifestyle and wonderful gifts so that I could feel worthy of her love. In some ways, it has served me well since I am very successful financially. But feeling like I must earn worthiness in this way is NOT WORTH IT! I tormented myself for so many years, not realizing that I was worthy, that I was a child of God, and that God was in me. That I am a living, breathing human being, and just by that, and that alone, I AM WORTHY. I am worthy of love, belonging, peace, joy, happiness, and love. (Just in case I didn't say that enough.)

It took me falling, failing, breaking down, and feeling like an utter and complete failure to start to feel worthy. I know that is paradoxical, but it was when I was so low that I had nothing to offer, that I began to see that I was loved just for me. I was almost 39 years old! I hope you don't have to wait that long, and if you are older than that, it is never too late. At that low point, I couldn't earn any money. My business was failing. I didn't know how to take care of my family, which is the most important thing in the world to me, and I was crying, stressed out, and felt like a wretched fool.

It was a Monday in early October 2009. The kids were at school, and I realized my business was failing, and we were out of money. I was face down on the floor of my home office, punching the carpet and cussing myself. "How could you be such a fool? How could you quit your good job, lose your retirement savings in a business, and now not be able to feed your family?! You are a f*&#ing idiot! You are so stupid and so reckless and such an idiot! What were you thinking?" I was crying and raging at myself at the same time, and it went on for quite a while. I felt a loving, confident touch on my shoulders and heard my wife say, "Come with me, Honey." "But I can't," I replied, "I must figure this out! I have to find a way to make money so we can pay the bills and eat. I have to! I have to!"

"Not right now, you don't. And you can't figure anything out in this state. Come with me, darling, come with me."

I slowly raised myself off the floor and grabbed my handkerchief to wipe away the snot from my nose and mouth. I started to explain the situation we were in financially, but she calmly and lovingly quieted me, took me by the hand, and gently led me out of my office into the family room. There, she had the shades lowered, popcorn and hot chocolate on the coffee table, and "It's a Wonderful Life" queued up on the TV. She led me to the couch, put her arm around me, and pressed play as I started crying again. We watched the movie that we both love so much, and at the end, it hit me.

At that moment, I was unable to do any of the things I thought I had to do to earn Tonya's love, and SHE LOVED

ME! She told me so over and over again until I got it. I couldn't give her anything. I was completely broken and didn't even know how to pay the bills, and she loved me. I couldn't EARN any love in any way, and she loved me. I was a failure, and she loved me. I lost all the things that I thought I needed to have or be to be loved, and she loved me—so completely, so deeply—anyway. This is the same unconditional love that God gives us all the time, but I couldn't see that until I experienced it from her. That is when I started to see that I don't have to earn love—that I am worthy. I started doing incantations while I was running every day, speaking strongly, "I am worthy! I am worthy!" again and again. It still took a year or so to sink in completely, and there are times I still struggle with it today, but on the deepest level, I know that I am worthy, and it brings peace to my life. That was not complete until I felt that same love from God.

That was the other realization that I had during that time: GOD loves me, too, even more completely and more deeply than any human could. In fact, it was God's perfect love that was flowing through Tonya that day. And if God loves me that much, I must be worthy. Years later, my 12-step sponsor used the example of my beloved dogs, asking how much I love them, how much they earn that love, and how much they produce. I love them tremendously, and they produce nothing. God loves us like that, but so much more. How do you know God loves you, you might ask. I don't know how I know, and I do know. I think it is that anytime I do as it says in Psalms 46:10—"Be still and know that I am God"— I feel God's presence, and it brings me peace and joy.

Whenever I bring my attention inward, into my body, and feel the presence of being of God within me, I feel peace, and that is how I know God loves me. It also tells us in the Bible (John 3:16) that God so loved the world (us/you/me) that he gave his son for us. John 4:16 reminds us again, "And so we know and rely on the love God has for us. God is love. Whoever lives in love lives in God, and God in him." Finally, in John 15:13, we are told again: "Greater love has no one than this, that he lay down his life for his friends," which is what God did for us in Jesus.

THIS IS THE MOST IMPORTANT MESSAGE IN THIS BOOK. YOU ARE WORTHY! You have the skills to handle the challenges of life, and you are worthy of enjoying all the good things that life has to offer. You have received God's grace simply by being human. You don't need to earn love or earn God's grace. In fact, the Bible says in Ephesians 2:8-9 that you can't earn God's grace by good works; it is freely given to all who believe in Him. Simply by being human, you are worthy of all the good that life has to offer. And as we journey through life's ebbs and flows, let us remember that understanding God's love is not a destination but a journey, where each step forward enriches our souls and draws us closer to the heart of the divine. In this journey, every moment of realization, every act of kindness, and every challenge overcome is a testament to the depth of His love for us. I hope and pray that you feel and know this from the beginning and don't have to go through the suffering I did in my first 40 years to start to feel worthy.

Summary:

- Know you are worthy and belong just by being born, just by being a child of God. It is a birthright!

- You don't have to, and can't, earn love. If it is earned, it isn't unconditional love.

- Your gifts can only be brought forth when you know you are worthy. Know that and share your gifts with others!

Chapter 2:
You Are Loved!

"When you know how much God is in love with you, then you can only live your life radiating that love."

~ *Mother Teresa*

AMEN! You are so loved! By me. By your mom. (I am writing this directly to my children, whose parents and grandparents are still alive. If yours are not, they still love you from the other side. If you are estranged from your parents, they still love you, but they may not be good at showing it. I know what that is like. You are not alone.) You are loved by your grandparents on both sides. You are loved by your siblings. You are loved by your 20 aunts and uncles. You are loved by your 14 cousins. You are loved by your friends. You are loved by your dogs and cats. You are loved by so many. I could write this list to cover the whole page. You are loved. Do you know you are loved? Do you know that I love you more than it is possible to describe in words? I love you, yes, to the moon and back and around the sun and THIS much with my arms wide open until they touch back behind me. I never knew it was possible to love this much, until I had children, until I had you. You are loved more than words can say, more than money can buy, more than any career or fame. You are so loved that Mom and I would do anything for you that would help you have a better life. You are that loved, safe, and cared for. And you always will be. God also loves you so much that he gave his only son for you. You are that loved.

And you are that loved no matter what you do. It is completely disconnected. You don't have to earn any love. Nothing you can do or not do can make you loved any more or any less by God or by your family. Think about how you love your pets. Do they have to do anything to earn that love? No! They don't produce anything. They don't make money. They don't have to achieve. And you love them completely. God loves you like that and ten times over. As St. Augustine said, "God loves us as if there were only one of us."

I must tell you a little story here. Alex, this one is about you. We had tried to have kids for a long time, about 5 years, with no luck. We finally decided to adopt, and it was a very long process of paperwork, money, and waiting. It was tedious! Thankfully, Tonya did most of it. During this period, we were still wondering what it would be like to adopt. Would we have the same feelings for an adopted child as people have for biological children? Then we finally got a little video of this baby they were proposing for us to adopt. I still remember that night as if it were yesterday. We were living in Germany and sitting on the red, blue, and green couch watching the TV inside that brown amour that holds your video game TV today. We put in this little tape, and there you were, Alex, a tape of a little baby lying in a crib. It was only a few minutes long, and I knew at once that you were our son and I loved you so deeply and so completely from the first second I saw you in that video. I couldn't believe it was possible to love someone I had not even met that much. I had not even met you and loved you so deeply and completely as if we had been together for 20 years. If you had told me I would feel that way so quickly, I would not have believed you. I would have said that was impossible. And yet, here it was happening to me. It blew me away! It was the deepest, purest love I had ever felt towards someone I had not even met. That is how loved you are. All of you. I had the same experience when you were born, Sawyer. And the same feeling, Kayli, when they first handed you to us in China, you were wearing that Santa Claus suit and sweating profusely. You are all loved that deeply and have been since we first laid eyes on you.

Do you feel it? Do you know it? Do you love yourself that much? Do you see the miracle that you are?

This love is not a hiding place, but a springboard. It is not a dead end but a runway. It is not a love that constrains but a love that launches. It gives you roots, so you always know where you are from and who you are, and that you are always safe...and wings, so that you can go explore the world, both inside you and out. It gives you a safety net, not to stay in, but that is there to catch you when you fall, so that you have the safety to dare greatly, to live the life that you imagined, to shoot for the moon knowing that if you miss, you are still loved, and that love will catch you. It is a base for you to jump off to do more good in the world. You stand on the shoulders of all those who love you, especially Mom and me, to have the wings, the freedom to do more, to love more, to give more, to be more, to explore more, and ultimately to love more from the starting point of love, all this love for you.

This is a love that you can't earn and can't destroy. It is a constant love from all those who love you and from God. It is there, no matter what. It is there when you have your biggest accomplishments and your biggest mistakes. It is there when you feel worthy of it and when you don't. It is there when you are kind and when you are mean. It is always there. It is a love that we and God choose to give you.

Summary:

You are loved by God and many others completely and unconditionally, just as you are. There is nothing you can do that could ever change that. Do you know you are loved like that? Do you feel it? This is what matters the most. If you struggle with it, think of someone or a pet that you love, who makes you smile, just thinking about them. Know that they love you like that, too. I love you. And God loves you even more. And the family and friends you are close to love you like that, too. Rest on that. Breathe it in deeply and know that you are loved. In a later chapter, Love Wins, we will give more tools on how to fully love yourself, others, and your life.

Chapter 3:
Connect to Your Center, to God

"Truth is the offspring of silence and meditation."

~ Isaac Newton

Now that you know you are worthy and that you are loved, the most important thing you can do in your life is to connect to your center, to God, to the intelligent higher power that conducts the universe. It doesn't matter what you call it; Being, God, Inspiration, Wisdom, Presence, Universe, Intuition, Higher Self, Center, or, as is in all Twelve-Step Recovery, Higher Power. But it is crucial that you connect to It. This may be the most important thing, but I have found it is hard to do this if I don't know that I am loved and that I belong. So that is why those two are first.

What if I don't believe in God? That is OK. The steps you will take to connect with whatever It is are the same as if you did believe. And you don't have to believe in It to connect with It. You can just call it your still voice, or your inner self if you want. And you can connect with it at whatever age. The breath is the simplest and fastest way to connect with It. The gateway to It is always through the present moment, and the fastest way to connect with the present moment is the breath.

Breathe:

Whatever is going on, stop and take a very deep breath in and an extremely slow breath out, as slowly as possible, and completely as possible. Then breathe in deeply again to the count of 4 and hold that for a count of 4. Then breathe out slowly to a count of six and hold it for a count of 2. It looks like this, "In, 2, 3, 4. Hold, 2, 3, 4. Out, 2, 3, 4, 5, 6. Hold, 2. In, 2, 3, 4...." Doing this only 3 times will bring you into the present moment and into your body, which will connect you with this Higher Intelligence. Obviously, the more you do this breathing, the stronger the connection will be. Three sets of 10 breaths like this are ideal and twice per day. And I don't do that much very often. But I do use it any time I am feeling stressed, anxious, scared, or adrenalized. Nervous about the interview? Breathe like this. Scared of calling the one that attracts you to ask them out? Breathe. Do you want to get clear on what you should do? Breathe. About to walk into the biggest presentation of your life? Breathe. Nervous about asking your parents? Breathe! It is in these moments that I stop and follow this breathing. When I do, the event goes well. When I don't, it usually comes off the rails a little bit. Breathe to connect.

Meditate:

If you have more time, the most reliable way to connect is to turn that breathing into a meditation. Keep your attention on your breath and continue that count 10 times. Then let the breath come back to normal, easy breath, but focus on it. Keep your attention on your breath as it moves in and out. When you have completed 1 inhale and one exhale, count 1, and then second in and out, count 2. Continue this up to 10 and then back down to 1. Your mind will wander. When it does, just gently bring it back to the breath and count where you left off or start over. Continue this for 10 or 15 minutes, ideally twice per day, and you will start to feel calmer and more centered immediately after the first meditation. A few weeks of daily practice, and you will start to feel more present and calmer most of the time. Meditation is any time you tune out what is going on around you and put your attention fully on what Jeff Warran calls a home base. Anything you are sensing with one of your five senses, most often the breath. And when your attention drifts away, it will bring it back. This opens the window to God. Most of the time when my mind wanders, it is thinking about what I am doing next, when I am going to school, what I am going to eat, or who I am meeting. But sometimes, out of the stillness comes pure inspiration. Some spark of what to do, how to solve a relationship issue, what the answer to a problem is, or what to write at a point where I had been stuck. This is when you know you have connected to It. Anytime you feel peace and calm, that is "The peace of God that surpasses all understanding" coming through. It surpasses all understanding because you can experience it even during a crisis. From that calm, inspiration strikes. It doesn't happen very often, and when it does, capture the inspiration in a journal. (More about that later.) I have also noticed that meditation is most effective in nature. I feel the calmest, most peaceful, and have the highest number of inspirations when I meditate in nature, which is our next subject.

Nature:

Today, there is much written about the benefits of forest bathing. It has many, and it doesn't even need to be that fancy. Get outside where there are more plants than buildings! Even look outside. A study done at the University of Michigan shows that people who walked outside in nature versus in the cityscape scored better on tests afterward. Not only that, but people who just looked at pictures of nature on a screen did better than those who looked at pictures of cityscapes. Surround yourself with nature, even if it is just pictures. If you can, go outside. Take your dog for a walk. Do homework outside. Take the business call walking outside or even make it a walking meeting. Bounce on your trampoline. Walk barefoot in your backyard. There are many studies now also showing the benefits to young people of being "free-range kids." That is, children who would go outdoors after school, and the parents would simply tell them to be home for dinner. These kids spend time outdoors, connecting with nature, daydreaming, playing, and connecting with friends. All of these are made better by being outside. For me, the connection to inspiration in nature is the strongest at sunrise. I love being out riding my bike, running, or simply sitting on the deck or beach watching the sunrise. Meditating there compounds the connection and frequency of inspiration. Even if you are driving, turn the radio off, don't answer the phone, and just notice the nature around you, the trees, the sky, and the fields rolling out in front of you. For a deep connection with your center, spend 3 days in the complete wilderness, off technology, and immersed in nature for all your senses, sight, touch, smell, sound, and taste. I think of two great examples of that. First, Sawyer and I did a 12-day backpacking trip at the Boy Scout Camp, Philmont, NM, when he was 17. On his 18th birthday, I asked him what the highlight of his life was so far, and that adventure was it. It was difficult, it was uncomfortable, but it was a grand adventure and connected us to nature, to God, and to each other. The other example is from the summer of 2023, when all 5 of my siblings, 5 nieces and nephews, and 1 brave sister-in-law joined for a 6-day backpacking journey in the Bob Marshall Wilderness in Montana. Each day, we hiked until we found a flat enough place to set up camp that was always by water, usually a stream. We had no cell phone signal and only used our phones for cameras by agreement. The sounds were the breeze, birds, and running water. There weren't even any airplanes. We used all our senses, feeling the breeze, sun, and the cold stream water for a dip at the end of the day on our skin, tasting the wild huckleberries, smelling the fir trees and abundant wildflowers, and seeing all the majestic beauty of the mountains, trees, and flowers. We also engaged our emotional senses by connecting and hugging each other. By the end of the third day, I was completely at peace, happy, and maintained that for the rest of the trip. Everything simply flowed. I had many inspirations, which I captured in my journal each day. That leads to the next ways to connect with the Self: silence, play, and journaling.

Silence:

Silence is the window through which we hear God. It calms our minds, releases stress, and allows us to hear that Inner Voice, which we will talk about in the next chapter. And it can be hard to embrace silence. We are so used to being engaged all the time! We have phones that bring the entire world to our pockets and headphones that can always be playing our favorite music, podcast, or book. We are addicted to this constant stimulation. So, it can be hard to let it go, especially for the first time or the first 5-10 minutes. Our brain wants that little dopamine hit of being engaged, of always processing, of always being on. What works for me is to time it for only 15 minutes. I often do this while driving or running. Just turn everything off and be still. I always squirm a little in the beginning as I go through the mini withdrawals of stopping the stimulation. But I always feel more centered at the end of those 15 minutes. Additionally, incorporating brief moments of silence before starting your day or before meals can gradually accustom your mind to embrace stillness, making those longer periods of silence feel more natural and rewarding. Again, silence in nature compounds the good effects. In this silence, we can also hear from Intelligence. When we do, it's great to capture that in a journal. So always have a small journal in your backpack.

Journaling:

Journaling is a great way to capture inspiration, for sure, and please use it for that. The best way to journal is with pen and paper, but really, the best way is the way you can do it daily. My main journaling is audible, on my phone, that I do first thing every morning. I pray and reflect on yesterday, what I did well and could do better, and what I am grateful for now. I check in to see what I am feeling, where I am feeling it in my body, and who's feeling it, what part of me is feeling it. I then ask that part what it wants to say. (For more on this, please look at the great work on parts therapy by Dr. Richard Schwartz.) Whatever part comes up, the part of me that responds to that part is my Center, the "capital S" Self. This is also a window to God or Knowing. If the feeling that came up was not joy or peace, I start over after the discussion and repeat until I am feeling joy or peace. I then ask God what to "be" that day, and what presence God wants me to hold. Then, what to do that day and record both of those on my daily action plan. This is my most consistent way to connect to God. You can learn more about my morning process on my website, artblanchford.com, or on my *Life in Transition* Podcast, Episode 8. All of this is done audibly on my phone. I also write on paper anytime I am backpacking or on retreats, especially silent ones. This writing process often starts from somewhere outside me, and I read what I have written as I go. It often turns into a conversation with God where I get a very clear direction. The most recent example of this was on a guided retreat hiking through the Alps for 7 days, where we were set alone on a mountain with only water, a jacket, and a journal for an undetermined time with no watch or phone. My mind went crazy, so I meditated and then started to journal and got so much clear direction, one of which was to finish this book this year. That is why I am sitting on my back deck, writing right now. Journaling is a powerful tool to both connect and record what comes from that connection.

Read:

Read wisdom literature. When your mind is calm after meditation or silence, read the Bible or any other book of wisdom. Spend 15 minutes a day reading things that inspire you. See the Resources List in the appendix for more ideas. Spending time in this absorbing wisdom in this way can bring you closer to God and will give you inspiration. Here are a few books to read that encompass a broad spectrum of wisdom:

- "The Sacrament of the Present Moment" by Jean-Pierre de Caussade, Kitty Muggeridge, et al. - shows us how to let go and let God work in our lives by being fully present in the moments he gives us.

- "The Untethered Soul" by Michael Singer - shows us the simple, everyday steps to healing ourselves and living life with a deep presence and sense of gratitude.

- "The Book of Joy" by Dalai Lama and Desmond Tutu - A profound dialogue between two spiritual giants, exploring the nature of joy amidst life's challenges.

- "Man's Search for Meaning" by Viktor E. Frankl - A psychiatrist's memoir of surviving concentration camps with lessons on finding purpose in pain, emphasizing spiritual survival.

- "The Seven Spiritual Laws of Success" by Deepak Chopra - A practical guide that blends physics and philosophy to explain how success can be achieved through understanding the natural order of the universe.

- "Autobiography of a Yogi" by Paramahansa Yogananda, Ben Kingsley, et al. - reveals the energy behind all existence and the complete connection to God of the Holy from India. This book moved me.

Play:

Play comes up for me when I think about younger children connecting to God, but it is just as meaningful for adults, too. Play is a wonderful way to forget oneself, to stop the chattering mind, the incessant inner dialogue. When we stop it, we connect to God, to the Source. Play often brings up joy, which is also a connection to God. I could see it in my three children when they were younger. They would lose themselves in play, and the centeredness I felt just witnessing it was powerful. As I recover from workaholism, I have started to learn the simple joys of real play. I had many adventures before, but mostly I turned them into work with goals and kept my mind busy calculating the outcome, the finish. That is not play. Play is getting lost in the simple joy of something only for its sake, for joy. I find it often now, bouncing on the trampoline or listening to music, especially with the windows down in the truck, and doubly especially if I am singing along. Singing and dancing are wonderful ways to play. It can also be running fast down a hill just for the fun of it, like when I was a child. This simple, joyful play brings me into the present and into my heart and body, out of my busy mind, and there I find joy and sometimes Inspiration. It connects me to Self, to God. Try it and see what works for you.

Chapter Summary/Key Takeaways:

Connecting to a Higher Power, or whatever you call it, is

essential to living a joyful and meaningful life. It guides all that I am and all that I do. Earlier in life, it did not make sense to me. What is God? I wanted to do what I wanted to do, not what God wanted me to do. So, I pushed back against this for a long time. My life looked good on the outside. I had money, a family, a lovely home, professional respect, adventure, and fitness. And I was dying inside and didn't even know it. I was constantly stressed and in fear. It was so pervasive that I didn't even know it was there. I thought that was just the way it was. I was later diagnosed with General Anxiety Disorder. And my body forced me to slow down to heal. My energy was so low that I spent most of my time in bed for several months and was diagnosed with chronic fatigue syndrome. When I had no other choice, I started to let go and let God in. Now I see clearly what I truly desired was joy, peace, contribution, health, adventure, love, belonging, and community, and those all come from God, from this Intelligence I still do not fully understand. I don't understand it, but I now have many examples of how good my life is when I connect to God, when I listen to the small, still, quiet voice to guide everything.

So how do I connect? It starts with slowing down and making space. The first step of that is to breathe deeply and then focus on your breath, bringing you back to your body, to the present moment. Do that anytime you are feeling stressed, anxious, or disconnected. Meditation is the next step. Sit quietly and focus on your home base; the breath is the most common one. And do that for at least 10 minutes daily. This can be a form of silence, which is another way to slow down and connect to the present. Step off the attention economy superhighway. Set down your phone. Turn off any noises you can and be in silence. The positive effects of silence are compounded by being in nature, especially at sunrise. The magic of nature is immediate; with 3 days of full immersion, it is transformative. Play, sing, dance, and move in ways that you forget yourself. This can be as simple as singing along to a song or running fast down a hill. Read wisdom literature or even listen to an audiobook or podcast from Sage. Finally, journal. Write to process your thoughts and open a portal to inspiration. And write or audio record the inspirations you get from these other connections. Writing after any healing process, meditation, silence, or time in nature is a great way to connect and process. Use these tools to connect to your higher power and see how your life magically transforms. Mine has, and I hope you don't have to wait until midlife to get there. Having made the connection, in the next chapter, we will explore how to hear that voice and act on it.

Chapter 4:
Listen to Your Inner Voice

"Trust God from the bottom of your heart; don't try to figure out everything on your own. Listen for God's voice in everything you do, everywhere you go; he's the one who will keep you on track."

~ Proverbs 3:5-6 in The Message

Do I have an inner voice? Yes, everyone has one. What is your inner voice? Do you ever think, "Should I do that?" Do you ever feel your intuition nudging you to go one way even if your friends are saying to go another? Do you ever feel God is leading or calling you to do something? Some people call this intuition. Some call it God's calling or voice. Some call it your true voice. Some call it your subconscious. In business, we often call it going with your gut. It is that small, quiet voice or thought that comes up when you are trying to make a decision that nudges you in a certain direction. So, we know we have an inner voice. How do we listen to it? How do we tune into it? Sometimes it will speak clearly, like when a group of friends or colleagues is trying to make a decision, and you have this knowing rise up about what is right and wrong. You must listen. You must have the courage to follow that voice and share what you know. Usually, it is a still, quiet voice, so the first thing is to still the other chatter in the mind. How do you do that? The best way is to be completely in the present moment, not thinking about something else. To do that, take three deep breaths through your nose and out through your mouth. If you can, step away from your routine for a few minutes. Best if you can go outside and be in nature. Feel the air, breeze, and sun on your skin. Really notice it. Feel your body. If you have time, sit quietly, close your eyes, and breathe for 5 or 10 minutes just focusing on your breath or some other physical sensation in your body. Then see what rises. What inspiration comes to you after not focusing on it? If nothing comes up, ask, "What is the right action here?" and wait and see what comes up. When it does come up, when you have a clear sense of what to do, you must listen to it. You must follow that sense. For example, you are in a group of friends, and one starts talking down about another friend who is not there. Your inner voice says, "That's not true. Speak up and defend that friend." There is a moment of choice. Do we have the courage to speak up for what we know is right? Our job is to follow that sense;that inner voice that we know is right. If we don't, we will start to try to justify why we didn't. That is the voice that says, "But these friends might not like me," or "I don't know that other person very well anyway, so it doesn't matter." This is justification and not your inner voice, and we must not follow that one. That is the voice that leads to separation and seeing others as lower than ourselves.

Here are a few recent examples from my life. When I was packing for our 21st anniversary trip to Las Vegas, where we were also going hiking, I felt that inner voice nudging me to take the anti-chafing Body Glide with me, and I almost did. Then my logic, or justification, kicked in and said, "You will not need this. We are not doing any real tough hikes, and even a 10-mile one won't cause chafing since it is low humidity there. I will leave it here. Pack light!" With this justification, I didn't bring it. I listened to the justification instead of my inner voice. MISTAKE! On our first hike, I didn't need it, but Tonya did. Now I knew why the small voice spoke up. That is the tricky part; we often don't know why, so we try to justify it, but we don't need to. We just need to listen.

Later in that trip, I was loading my running backpack to go for my 12-mile run, and there was a small plastic grocery bag there. I heard that small voice again, "Take it with you." I thought, "Why will I need that?" Then I thought, "Yes, it is a long run and, in the desert, and I might need to use the bathroom and should leave no trace, so maybe I should bring it." So, I did take it. I listened to my inner voice and my justification, not leaving a trace, but picking up others' trash along the trail. Again, I didn't know why, but I followed the inner voice, and the why became clear later. My justification was wrong.

Finally, on the third day of a business trip this week, I was out running early as usual, when I felt the addiction of multi-tasking, feeling like I should be doing more than just running. I thought, "Who should I call?" Immediately, I heard that still voice, God's voice, whispering, "Let it be, Art. Enjoy the stillness of the morning." My logic immediately kicked in, "but you haven't talked to the children in a few days. And it is a long run, and you will need to talk with them. And it is quieter now, and I am not sweaty, and I don't have headphones, and, and, and..." In that moment of choice, I listened to the logic, and the justification, and decided to call. Even with the "good" justification of connecting with family, it is still justification and not listening to God's voice. I called my middle son, Sawyer, on FaceTime, but it somehow rang on my wife's phone, and I woke her up. Douhhhhh! I wish I had listened to my inner voice, not the justification.

It works on bigger decisions too. For example, when I was stressed about what to do next in my career back in 2000, I really couldn't decide. We were living in TN, working out of Detroit, traveling too much, and trying to have kids. I had been struggling with the decision for a long time. Then we went to Hawaii for our fifth anniversary, and I ran each morning, clearing my mind and letting things go. The next week, I was on a flight from Nashville to Utah that was chasing the sunset on one side of the plane and great thunderstorms on the other. It was extraordinarily beautiful. I was reading Dan Millman's book, *The Way of the Peaceful Warrior*, and was completely still and in the present. With such quiet and beauty, the still voice seemed quite loud and coming from nowhere said, "Move to Germany!" "Move to Germany?" I asked. "Really?" Logic kicked in. Tonya had a good job in Tennessee, and I had planned to be the plant manager of a local plant. We had just bought a house a couple of years ago and had just bought a new Miata that we couldn't take with us. All the justification and logic said not to go, but the inner voice was so clear that I listened to it instead. There was a small job open in Germany at Autoliv, where I worked. I applied for it and didn't get that one, but a few weeks later, I was approached by the president of Autoliv Germany, who said he had heard I was interested in coming to Germany and he had a big job he would like me to consider. I interviewed and felt the job was too big, but I got it and moved to Germany for 3 years. Those 3 years launched my career!

In 2021, I wanted to quit my corporate job, but I was so afraid I would not survive financially. I prayed about it, and God was very clear that he was going to provide, but my logical mind couldn't accept that, and I asked God HOW would he provide. He said I could just trust him. I know I should, but I said, "I am an engineer with anxiety, I really need to know." He replied, "If you really must know, it will be in real estate." "Real estate! Are you kidding me? I don't know anything about real estate." My logical voice said. "Yes, real estate. Leave it alone." I trusted God and this inner voice, quit my job, and returned to physical and spiritual health. And a little over a year later, the real estate market went up like crazy, and we sold our farm for more than 3 times what we had bought it for 10 years earlier, and double what it was worth at the time I heard my inner voice.

Summary:

Occasionally, that quiet, internal guidance is crystal clear; other times, achieving a state of complete mental tranquility is necessary to perceive its subtle nudges. Once this inner voice makes its presence known, we are called to attentively listen and act upon its direction, without the compulsion to unravel the 'why' behind its counsel. It is about choosing to heed this gentle whisper over the louder, more persistent voices of rationalization that emerge in its wake. This act of trust demands courage, for the path it suggests may not always appear logical or straightforward. Yet, it is by consistently surrendering to this small voice, time and again, that our lives begin to unfold in wondrously unexpected ways, imbued with a sense of enchantment and deeper purpose.

This reflection on the inner voice shows how listening to our intuition can change our lives in many ways—personally, at work, and spiritually. It encourages readers to get in touch with their deepest selves, moving beyond common knowledge. By trusting and following our gut feelings, we open the door to personal growth and happiness, highlighting the beautiful path that unfolds when we listen to what's inside us.

Chapter 5:
Find Your Adventure

"The big question is whether you are going to be able to say a hearty yes to your adventure?"

~ *Joseph Campbell*

One of our best and hardest jobs to do as human beings, let alone as we are growing up, is to find what really juices us, what we want to be and do. What is OUR grand adventure? What is my passion? And most people never get there. They get busy doing the life they think they are supposed to be doing. They are busy getting good grades, going to college, and getting a good job. Then, getting married. Getting promoted. Raising children and paying the bills. There is nothing wrong with any of these things, but it doesn't automatically answer the biggest question posed above. "Will you show up for your grand adventure?" To show up for it, you must know what it is. You must find your grand adventure, your passion, what calls to you, what inspires you, what God has called you to do. This is the main purpose of your 2nd and 3rd decades on the planet. From birth to age 10 is just about being a beloved child. From age ten to twenty, it is about exploration and education. Which subjects call to you? What lights you up? What excites you? Your twenties are about trying your hand at many different things. It is about exploring the world and yourself. You see a hill in the distance that intrigues you. You go for it and hike up to the top, and realize it is not a hill for you, or maybe even halfway up, you realize it is not for you. It is not because the hike is hard, as anything worthwhile is hard, but you are not inspired. It no longer calls to you, even if it pays well.

This is why many people get stuck. They get used to having a little money and sell out on their passions to keep it. So, go for your passions before you even start earning much money.

"There are two goddesses in your heart," he told them. "The Goddess of Wisdom and the Goddess of Wealth. Everyone thinks they need to get wealth first, and wisdom will come. So, they concern themselves with chasing money. But they have it backward. You have to give your heart to the Goddess of Wisdom, give her all your love and attention, and the Goddess of Wealth will become jealous, and follow you. Ask nothing from your running, in other words, and you'll get more than you ever imagined."— US Olympic Running Coach, Joe Vigil, quoted by Christopher McDougall in *Born to Run: A Hidden Tribe, Superathletes, and the Greatest Race the World Has Never Seen*

This says it so well. Go for your passions first. So, if this mountain no longer inspires you, walk back down. Don't be afraid of going backward, going down the mountain to climb another one. This is a mistake that I made, and many make. We get up the mountain in a way where we have status, visibility, some income, and success, and we are afraid of losing face by climbing back down, by starting over. It is hard on our ego, so we continue for all the wrong reasons. We are afraid of looking bad. Well, if you continue up a mountain that is not for you, you will eventually have to come down from a higher, more visible place. In that "wrong way" of looking at it, you would be a "bigger failure." But it is not a failure, as the point of your twenties is to explore. Maybe the purpose of climbing the first mountain was to see another mountain that lights your fire. You climb down, so you can go climb the one that inspires you. Don't be afraid to do this many times in your 2nd and 3rd decades. I can tell you from personal experience that if you don't do it, then it will come back to you in midlife. If you are lucky and courageous, you will answer the call then, climbing down, maybe very far down off a high mountain you have worked for decades to climb. But you have more perspective now and realize life is short, and you want to find your passion while you have this window. Most still won't answer the call and will continue, as Benjamin Franklin said, "To live lives of quiet desperation." The advantage of climbing many mountains when you are in your teens and twenties is that you will have longer on the mountain you love, your passion, than if you wait until you are 50, as I did.

Finding this passion or these passions for yourself is one of your main jobs of growing up and evolving as an adult. Try different things and see how they feel. There are countless activities to take part in as you grow up, from gymnastics to robotics clubs, from music to rugby or archery, to JA BizTown, Junior Achievement's summer camp focused on teaching business to students. While earning Merit Badges in Scouts, you can experiment with a variety of activities to see what you like the best. You can notice what types of things you like to do, studying or reading by yourself, socializing with friends, being in front of the group speaking, or supporting from backstage. Do you like playing with our dog Dudley or taking care of your bearded dragons, or would you rather cook, work on the car, race a car, program a computer, create music or art, or comfort others through teaching or healing, or lead a business, run, or ski, or design a game? For all of you, whether in your teens or sixties, the most important way to find your inspiration is to be still and listen to the quiet inner voice, as we discussed in Chapter 3. Go back to those journals and see what you have written. See what speaks to you, what you are curious about. After that, there are also lots of tests and books that can help you learn what you might be good at and enjoy doing. *What Color is Your Parachute*, the classic book by Richard Nelson Bolles, can help you find what you love. The CliftonStrengths assessment can help show you what innate strengths you have.

https://store.gallup.com/c/en-us/1/cliftonstrengths

Mistakes:

Be careful to use your strengths in service of your passions, not just to "do something you are good at," which is another mistake many people make. Finally, don't avoid things because you are afraid or think you might fail or look foolish. Everyone is a beginner when they begin. Everyone fails. Everyone has fears. Be driven by inspiration and passion, not fear.

I am still looking at ways to spend more time connecting with, teaching, and leading people since I love it so much. That is why I am writing this book: to help you, my three children, and hopefully any others, to find your gifts and then share them with the world. It is not just for you. The world needs your gifts and your creativity; it needs your unique offering. Not going through the discomfort of finding your grand adventure, your purpose, your passion, prevents you from bringing your gifts to us, to the ones who would receive help from it. And we are waiting for your gift. From that perspective, giving in to fear or comfort or laziness is selfish. You are keeping your gift from the rest of us. You are hiding the beauty, keeping the flower from blooming. Not only are you keeping it from the rest of us, but you will also suffer later by not following your passion. Saint Thomas said it very well, "If you bring forth what is within you, it will save you. If you don't bring forth what is within you, it will destroy you." Avoiding bringing forth our passion and our gifts leads us to distractions and addictions that we turn to fill the hole left by not bringing forth our gifts, by not following our inspiration. These addictions will eventually destroy us or at least keep us stuck. My addiction was overworking. Yes, it looked good on the surface, and work is necessary for supporting my family and accomplishing any worthwhile goal. But I overdid it and hid in it as a way of avoiding my passions and gifts and my discomforts. It became my identity and a full-on addiction, and I am very grateful for my ongoing recovery in Workaholics Anonymous. I am now living my dream life, my grand adventure of learning from and teaching others via my *Life in Transition* Podcast and Intensives, my coaching and consulting, writing books, and my Friday Reflections Blog, and participating in and leading great outdoor adventures with my family and friends. I now have something I never thought I had before: time; time to be with, live life with, and support my family and friends in ordinary ways. When I do these things, which are my passions, I feel great and help many others as well. I feel purposeful, which gives me long-term joy.

This poem by George Bernard Shaw says it so well that I have had a framed copy in my office for decades.

This is The True Joy in Life –

The being used for a purpose recognized by yourself as a mighty one.

The being a force of nature instead of a feverish little clod of ailments and grievances, complaining the world will not devote itself to making you happy.

I am of the opinion that my life belongs to the whole community, and as long as I live, it is my privilege to do for it whatever I can.

I want to be thoroughly used up with I die, for the harder I work, the more I live.

I rejoice in life for its own sake.

Life is no brief candle to me.

It is a sort of splendid torch which I've got to hold up for the moment.

I want to make it burn as brightly as possible before handing it on to future generations.

When you overcome your fear and resistance, find this passion, this purpose, and use yourself for that, you will be fully alive, free, enthusiastic, and on fire. You will have deeper relationships, richer experiences, more purpose, and more of what you love. It will not be easy, as we will talk about in a later chapter, but you will have peace and confidence that comes no other way. And it is fun! Fulfilling a purpose recognized by ourselves as a mighty one is the deepest kind of joy.

Find what inspires you! For you, Kayli (at age 9), it may be gymnastics. I love seeing you so enthusiastic about that, and you are progressing fast. For you, Alex (at age 14), it may be working with animals, gaming, archery, gymnastics, music, or art. Keep looking, and when you find something you love, lean in, even if you are afraid or if it is hard. For you, Sawyer (age 11), it may be in connecting with and leading others, as you have a big heart and really love others and love leading, as well. Maybe it will be a caring profession like health care or ministry. Again, keep looking, noticing what makes you feel good after you have done it, and keep doing it. That is another key indicator. When you have completed something, look back on it and see how you feel about it now. Often, the things that seem tempting, fun, or appealing before you do them don't feel good in retrospect. Think of eating that second or third piece of cake, staying in bed all day, or watching that 4th episode on Netflix. When you are done with those things, you feel worse than before you started. Conversely, doing the thing that feels scary now or uncomfortable, like going over and saying something to the new kid in school or the one you are attracted to, or sitting down to write that paper or book, or going out for that run, or cleaning the house, will make you feel much better when you are done. Keep trying things and being uncomfortable until you find what you love.

Summary and Actions:

For you and for the good of all those you influence, find your passion! Say a hearty yes to your adventure. It is your job! It is your duty. For the gift of having this wonderful life you have been given, your part is to find your purpose and fulfill it with joy.

So, find your passions! There are many ways to do it, and the best way is to try many things you are curious about, even if fear comes up, even if you will be bad at it at first. Stop now and take deep, box breaths as described in Chapter 3. Get your journal and pen and write down 3 things you are passionate about. If that is too strong, then 3 things you are inspired by or at least curious about.

Things I am passionate about, or at least curious about.

1. _____

2. _____

3. _____

This is the first step on your grand adventure that will bring you everything. It will bring you stamina, persistence, wisdom, joy, rich relationships, provision, and simply the joy of being, which is the most important thing there is anyway.

These are other ways to find what you're passionate about that may be helpful:

1. Keep **a Passion Journal:** Beyond just listing things you're curious about, actively journal about experiences with new activities, how they made you feel, and any ideas they spark. This reflection can help clarify your passions.

2. Identify **Activities that Make You Lose Track of Time:** Pay attention to when you become so engrossed in an activity that time seems to fly by. These flow states can indicate areas of deep interest and passion.

3. Explore **New Environments**: Sometimes, a change of scenery or diving into a new environment can inspire new interests. Whether it's traveling, attending workshops, or exploring different cultures, new experiences can spark passion.

Chapter 6:
Fear Not!

"You can be fearful, but don't be afraid."

~ Ken Rideout, Elite endurance athlete at age 52

It is scarier to think about it than to do it. How I wish I knew that when I was 12, 18, or even 30 years old. Watching my son Sawyer at the top of his first steep, tree-lined ski run in deep powder, reminded me of this timeless lesson. He was frozen in fear. Looking back on it, he said, "The top was big and scary! The skiing was fun, and even the falling was fine. Getting up was hard, but not scary." I had the same experience when I dropped off the cornice the same day. I also still clearly remember my first time at the top of a blue ski run back in my 20s and how long I was frozen by fear. I was playing all these movies in my head about how I would crash and break a leg or arm, or maybe even be so out of control that I would end up crashing and dying. Once I started skiing, the fear went away. Action cures fear. It is always scarier to think about it than it is to do it.

The same applies to business. When I was 31 and a newly minted Global VP of a multi-billion-dollar automotive supplier, my mentor wanted me to reach out directly to the VP of Purchasing at General Motors for the first time. It was very scary for me. I was afraid. The fear stopped me for a few days. When I finally reached out, the fear abated. We did great business together, and we are still friends today, 20 years later. If I had stayed frozen by the fear, none of that would have happened. I had the same experience asking for a promotion or raise, asking my girlfriend to marry me, or deciding to have children. And each week, writing my blog or releasing a new episode of the *Life in Transition* podcast, I am afraid, thinking about it. And sometimes, the fear stops me for a while, and I put it off, which leaves me stuck in the fear. But as soon as I take the action, the fear disappears like magic. That is what Ken is talking about above. We will all feel fear, the coward and hero alike. But our job is not to give in to the fear, which he calls being afraid. If we want to live the life of our dreams, we will have to overcome fear all the time. We can feel it, but not be frozen by it, not be afraid.

As I told Sawyer when he was frozen at the top of the run, just go! It doesn't matter so much which line down the run you choose; taking action, any action, will abate the fear. The action, especially when the stakes are high, takes your full attention and brings you into the present, into the NOW, where fear can't live. Fear is only in the future.

Where is fear keeping you frozen? It is not the way we are meant to live. We all feel fear, the coward and the hero alike. The difference is that the hero (anyone who takes action anyway) is not afraid. That means she feels the fear, but she doesn't identify with it. She doesn't take it on as her state of being, which would keep her frozen. She feels the fear but dares to take the right action anyway. And by taking that action, the fear melts away.

Summary and Actions:

It is OK to feel the fear. We all do. Don't get frozen by

42

it. Act, and the fear melts away. Where are you frozen by fear right now? Write it down. What's the smallest action you can take to get started, to get over being afraid? What can you do to feel the fear and then do it anyway, or to mitigate the fear? Remember, every great journey begins with a single step, no matter how small. Embrace the idea that action breeds confidence, not the other way around. Consider sharing your fear with someone you trust; talking it out can diminish its power and make your next steps clearer. By acknowledging your fear and planning to confront it, you're already demonstrating courage. Now, take that small step forward. Let your action light the way and watch as the shadows cast by fear start to disappear. Can you take that smallest action now? If so, put the book down and do it. If not now, when can you do it? Grab your phone and schedule it in your calendar. Take action. It is the antidote to fear.

Chapter 7:
Go for It!

*"Whatever you can do, or dream you can, begin it!
Boldness [action] has genius, magic, and power in it…"*

~ Johann Wolfgang von Goethe

The key to overcoming fear is action. Begin! Take the first step. Make the call to your customer. Set up that meeting with your boss. Have that courageous conversation with your friend, colleague, or spouse. Sign up for that race, or class, and hire that coach. Point your skis down the run and go!

Look back at Chapter 5 now. You wrote down 3 things you are passionate about or at least curious about. What are those? What is the smallest action that would move you in the direction of that passion or curiosity? For example, I have long had a dream of running the Boston Marathon. I tried to qualify once twelve years ago and failed. I put it on the back burner and have had many other great adventures in the last decade. But it is still there. Recently, a new friend of mine, my age, just qualified for Boston. That re-ignited that passion, that dream. And it is much harder to qualify now than it was then. But I felt real inspiration to go for it. I followed the process of finding my voice from chapters three and four and got a clear "yes" that this is something I want to do. To qualify, I would have to take 1 hour off my current marathon time, almost 25%. That is a huge undertaking. But I didn't let fear stop me, and I didn't focus on the outcome; I just decided to take the smallest action,

44

which is the next step toward this passion. I called that friend and set up a lunch date to talk about it. That was all, the smallest action in the direction of my passion. When that day came, I took the next action, meeting him, and talking about his experience, and the key, he said, was to have a great coach, and he recommended two. Later that day, I took the next small step and reached out to both coaches. One came back to me that day. I took the next and the next actions, listening to him, registering for a qualifying race in April, and started following his training plan. I did all this in one week. I never figured out if I could qualify or not, or how many hours in total I would have to train. I didn't get stuck in analysis paralysis that I do in many areas of my life. I simply took the next small action that was in front of me. I focused on what I could control, and now I am well on my way. Will I be successful? I don't know if I will qualify for Boston. But I am taking the actions I can, and I know I will transform my health and fitness even if I don't qualify, and that is more exciting to me than actually running Boston. So, following this curiosity, this dream of running the Boston Marathon is, at a minimum, transforming my health and fitness, and maybe an epic marathon race too. I have many other places in my life where I haven't taken the actions for a very long time, and the window closed on some, but I have picked up others later, like this book. But it is not always possible to pick them up later, so it is better to act now. Another good example I see in my family right now is three of us learning Italian together. We didn't analyze or think about it for a long time. We had the inspiration and signed up on Duolingo. We each followed that training plan for as little as 3 minutes a day, but almost every day. Now we are speaking some Italian, and there are still 5 months before our trip there. It feels good to be learning another language together. If I had stopped and thought about the amount of work or how busy I was, I would never have gotten started.

Let's say one of your passions from your list in Chapter 5 is to go on a big hike. Start by getting in shape now. Take the action of taking your dog for a 20-minute walk. Don't start researching hiking boots. You don't need those yet, and it doesn't move you closer to being in shape for the hike. In another example, say you want to become a YouTuber about your passion for reptiles. Make a video with your phone and post it today. Act!

Ok, back to those three adventures or at least curiosities. Write them below with the singular smallest action you can take now to move in that direction.

Adventure 1:

    Action:

Adventure 2:

    Action:

Adventure 3:

    Action:

Put the book down and take those three actions now. Even if the action is just to put time in your calendar to follow up when the other party is available. Take action, not research and then action. Get started. See where that takes you. Now that you have discovered a few adventures, go for it!

Part 1 Summary:

You have now found your voice. You know you are worthy, and you are loved. That you belong as much as anyone else to the human race just by being a beloved child of God, which you are. From there, you have learned how to connect with God, your Inner Voice, and to slow down and be still enough to hear that voice. You have started on one of the main and ongoing purposes of your life, finding your grand adventure and saying yes to it. You are overcoming your fear by acting on your passions. This brings purpose and joy. Congratulations!

In Part 2, you will learn tools that will help you along this wonderful journey. They come from my personal experience and will help you "say a hearty yes to your adventure." My wish for you is that you can learn those now, whether you are still growing up or just still growing, and not waste more years avoiding the adventure God made just for you. I hope that you learn it faster than I did and can spend more of your life on your adventure.

PART 2: TOOLS FOR THE JOURNEY

Chapter 8:
Love Wins

"Love the Lord God with all your passion and prayer and intelligence and energy. Love others as well as you love yourself. There is no other commandment that ranks with these."

~ Jesus Christ in The Message, Mark 12:29-31

There is nothing above this. Love wins. Love is the answer. As Mother Teresa said, "There are no extraordinary works, just normal works done with extraordinary love." Love undergirds all good, all right action, all peace, all joy. Love wins. It has three parts: loving God, loving yourself, and then loving others as well as you love yourself.

For me, loving God comes first as it grounds and directs me each day. I start each day in prayer and connection with God and thanking him for his grace and care for me and my life right now. I also regularly write prayers and put them in my God Box. They often contain spontaneous outpourings of my love for God. If that is available to you, practice loving God daily. The best way is by being happy and grateful. But if that is not accessible to you right now, don't worry about it. Love yourself.

Truly, deeply love yourself. The most useful reference to this is the book *Love Yourself Like Your Life Depends on It*, by Kamal Ravikant. Its foundation is three simple but difficult practices. First is looking in the mirror and saying "I love you" or "I love myself" for 5 minutes. This was

49

really hard for me at the beginning, and I cried and laughed a lot. It really moved me. The second is to meditate for 5-10 minutes a day, silently saying "I love myself" on each inhale. And finally, using this question, "If I truly, deeply loved myself, what would I do in this situation?" These have guided me to start loving myself well. When I look at myself in the mirror now, I almost always break into a big smile, instead of the shame I usually felt before. Practice loving and being loving to yourself. Give yourself grace and understanding. Get rest, do things that nourish you, that bring you joy and peace. Be compassionate toward yourself.

Once you love yourself well, then love others as you love yourself. Give them that same grace and compassion. Always keep your heart open toward yourself and towards others. When you feel it starting to close, the anger or self-righteousness starting to come in, stop what you are doing. Don't speak! Breathe and remember to keep your heart open and keep feeling love for yourself and others. When you feel the defensiveness abate, then re-engage.

Here, I want to address all the parents out there. Frequently, people ask me for parenting advice. There are only two things I know for sure. Love wins, and you must be the adult in the relationship. I don't know everything else, but these are certain. So, in parenting, love is the foundation for everything else. And it must be complete, unconditional love that doesn't care about how the kids reflect on you at all. It only cares about what is best for the person you are raising. When your child acts out in public, love doesn't worry about what other people think. Love doesn't worry about how you will look. Love doesn't worry about being late or even being tired. Love opens your heart toward your child and is immediately and only in a caring mode for them. What is going on for them? What do they need? What is the highest and best for them? It doesn't get angry! It doesn't threaten. It is not weak either, but the motive is always what is best for the child and only what is best for the child.

Following is the story I shared in Episode 6 of the *Life in Transition* Podcast, which shows how I learned this the hard way at a monastery in the remote New Mexico desert. I hope you already know it or can learn from my experience, so you experience less suffering than I have.

Seeing my errors starkly, I was heartbroken and collapsed to my knees on the stone floor of my small room in this remote monastery. I wailed loudly for half an hour. Finally, after not speaking for 4 days, I spoke to Jesus, hanging on the cross in my room, asking, no, begging him to forgive me for seeing my kids as objects, not human beings, all these years, and for all the damage that had been caused.

Are your loved ones people or objects to you? Of course, they are people, you say, but don't answer too quickly. I would have said the same thing, but I would have been wrong.

Yes, I loved my children and checked all the boxes I thought I should be checking for proper care and development for them. But I was missing the most important one, and I didn't even know it. Five days of silence in a New Mexico desert helped me to see that. I'm looking at my journal that I wrote during that time in 2019, and I write, "I hate to admit it, but I have been trying to influence not just Alex, but all my kids to make my own life story turn out the way I wanted with me at the center, with me as the hero. Wow! Ouch! The truth hurts! What damage have I done to Alex, but also to Sawyer and Kayli?" That's what I wrote in my journal. And it was a difficult, transformative time and an amazing learning curve for me. It's so deep and it's still raw, even three and a half years later. I'll give you a little background. In the summer of 2019, I was number two in a public auto tech company running North America, China, and Korea. I had three teenage kids, two of whom were adopted, and one of whom had reactive attachment disorder. I was trying to be the *perfect* dad, husband, and corporate globetrotting executive, and son, and brother, and friend, and adventure athlete.

And I was about to collapse, but I didn't know it yet. I had planned to volunteer at an outdoor camp my daughter was going to, but she had injured her thumb and couldn't go. Now I was sitting on my back deck with my head in my hands, feeling bad for my daughter and feeling way too busy to be gone for 10 days to that camp anyway. I was completely overwhelmed by work and life and felt like I was about to collapse. At this point in my career, I was traveling around the world once a month and sometimes traveling for three weeks a month. Some friends in my men's group were going to the Monastery of Christ in the Desert in New Mexico, as they do every year. It sounded great, but I couldn't go when they were going. Even though I had been gone so much, my wife sensed how close to the edge I was and encouraged me to use those 10 days I'd blocked for the camp and go on a retreat somewhere. I couldn't manage 10 days completely off from work, but I decided on a five-day retreat to that Monastery.

I had never been to New Mexico and was really looking forward to the trip. I decided I would do a completely silent retreat and just meditate, journal, read the Bible, run, and hike. At this monastery, there is no Wi-Fi or cell signal, so my phone would only be for a camera. I would completely unplug for five whole days. As I packed, I was looking for *The Message* version of the Bible. I looked everywhere for it but couldn't find it. As I was frantically trying to get out the door to the airport, I made one last rushed search for the Message and I saw it, grabbed it, and stuffed it in my bag. It turns out it wasn't *The Message*, but a book of similar size, shape, and color called *Bonds That Make Us Free* by Terry Warner. Well, I thought, this must be the one God wants me to have. I had bought the book earlier on the recommendation of Ron Searle, who founded and was running the Arivaca Boys Ranch, where my oldest son, Alex, was staying, using equine and group therapy to overcome his reactive attachment disorder.

But it was big and thick, and I was busy, so I never read it. Alex healed a lot at the Ranch, as did the rest of the family at home while he was gone. We had to read and study *The Anatomy of Peace*, which Terry Warner also helped author. We were also required to join family and individual therapy. At the time, I was very nervous about that and thought, 'I didn't need therapy—that's for broken people.' Looking back now, I can't believe I used to feel that way. I have been in therapy almost weekly since then, and it has helped tremendously. Anyway, Alex had come home in December of 2018 and finished high school online with good grades and even had a job at Home Depot. He was doing well but started to spiral down rapidly. He again became very aggressive, angry, disrespectful, and threatened violence. Collaborating closely with a local therapist, we set the ground rules for our home and gave him three months to be in line with them. When he wasn't, I made him leave in March of 2019. I was proud of myself for staying calm as he cursed me and kicked and punched holes in the walls.

I asked if he wanted a sleeping bag. He asked why. I replied, "It's cold in March, and you might be living in your car." He reluctantly accepted it, and he was glad he had it after he was kicked out of his grandparents' house some days later. As he was getting in his car to leave, I asked if I could have a hug. He asked, "Why do you want a hug? I'm so pissed at you right now." I answered, "I want a hug because I don't know if I will ever see you again." I didn't get one. At that point, I felt he would end up in jail, dead, or we might never see each other again. That's how bad it was. My other two children were having issues, too. Sawyer, then 15, had gained 100 pounds, and Kayli had chronic pain in her thumb that had forced her to quit gymnastics, which was how she defined herself at this point in her life. And she had hives most days. This was all on top of a very demanding and contentious job, which is how I defined myself at that point in my life. All of this was swirling in my head as I made the long drive to and through Chama Canyon in the dark, arriving at the most remote monastery in the US, if not the world.

I checked into a small room with a small desk and a single bed, and no bathroom or AC. I found a leather medallion that signified silence and put it around my neck. I wouldn't speak until I found peace. And I didn't, which is amazing considering how much I love to talk ☺. I meditated, ran, read, wrote, hiked, contemplated, and watched the river and the amazing canopy of stars. I slept when I was tired, no matter what time of day. I didn't stress out about being awake in the middle of the night as I had at home, but I just went out and enjoyed the stars. I just let time unfold. It was incredibly freeing. I ate meals with the monks in silence and attended a few services. On my fourth day, when I was reading *Bonds That Make Us Free* on page 170, my world collapsed and expanded all at once. A woman was sharing how she was superwoman, doing everything for her kids. She earned money for them, cooked for them, loved them, hugged them, helped them with their homework, tucked them in, and went to their events. She was doing everything right, except she was not seeing them as human beings, but as objects.

She was working so hard to have the perfect life for herself and her children. But her children were accessories to her life, pieces of the puzzle surrounding her, with her at the center. They were not human beings in their own right, but just objects complementing her life. I saw myself starkly, and my world crashed down. I wept. I wailed loudly and messily for over half an hour. I used a whole towel, wiping the tears and snot away. Then I spoke. I asked, no, I begged Jesus, hanging on the wall over my bed, to forgive me, my lost self, for seeing my own children as objects, as accessories to my life, my "trying to be perfect" life, and for all the damage that had done. I was completely humbled and heartbroken and excited at the same time. I simultaneously felt so much grief for my lost time and lost ways, and so much hope for the future of our relationship, now that I saw the need to change. I cleaned myself up and went and talked to the Abbott for some advice. He listened patiently, kindly. When I was done, he said, "Art, thank God you have had this revelation now. You are the third man who has had this conversation with me, but you can do something about it. The other two were on their deathbeds. So, Thank God, and go do something about it."

I did. I changed my heart from one at war to one at peace. How did I have the change of heart? How did I make that transition? This is how, and it is THE most important thing in relationships. For all of you struggling with relationships out there, especially with children, busy executives, or busy parents, it is how we hold others, how our heart is toward them, that has the biggest impact. If I see someone else as an object, I can't have a great relationship with them, no matter what else I do. They feel that I'm seeing them as an object, as someone that is irrelevant, or an obstacle, or a vehicle. In my case, I saw my kids as a vehicle. I was using them to get what I wanted, to take me where I wanted to go, to have this perfect life. I had a picture of my life in my head that I thought would make me okay, would make me worthy of being loved. That picture was the perfect American Dream, where I would be a big success, make lots of money, and have a picture-perfect marriage and children. My children, much to my horror, now realizing this, were objects, pieces of the puzzle to make my life complete. They were accessories to my life and not their own human beings.

So how do you make the change? First, you must recognize how you really see them. I'll ask the question I asked in the beginning: do you see your loved ones as human beings whose dreams, desires, fears, and ambitions are just as valid as yours? Or do you see them as objects that are less important than yourself, whose cares and concerns and dreams matter just a little less than yours? How can you tell how you see them? If they do something embarrassing in public, is your first concern for them or for you? Is it about how they are feeling? What's going on with them? Or is it about how it will reflect on you? What will people think of you as a father, mother, or partner? If it is the latter, you see them as an object, and here's how you can change it.

First, from *Bonds That Make Us Free,* seeing other people as a problem is the problem. Let me restate that, seeing the other people as the problem is the problem. If I want to know what impact I am having on others, I only need to examine their response to me. If my child yells or lies to me a lot, I am somehow triggering that. How can I fix this problem if it's in myself, not them? It starts with understanding. The Bible says, to walk a mile in another man's shoes and Steven Covey writes, to seek first to understand and then to be understood. In *Bonds That Make Us Free*, Dr. Warner explains how to do that using the reconciliation exercise and collusion diagram. The reconciliation exercise is a way of seeing the truth about the other's qualities objectively and without offense. It's the data. Who are they, actually? I did this process for my relationship with my oldest son, Alex, 18 at the time. What I learned is that he is a real, complete human being with desires and dislikes just like my own, and he is lost and scared and without direction. I also learned that we have many things in common. He likes Legos, the game Talisman, music, fishing, or doing airsoft, and he likes doing them together. He doesn't want to grow up yet. He is scared. My question is how I can ease the transition for him, his life in transition. He doesn't understand the effect of his actions on others. How can I help him learn?

Those are things I learned once I looked at him objectively and saw what his qualities really are. The next step is the collusion diagram. The first question in the collusion diagram is how do I see what the other is doing? In this case, how do I see what Alex is doing? I saw that he was bullying his siblings, stealing, cussing, disrespecting me, being really mean, intentionally hurting his family, threatening violence, making our home a minefield, refusing to do even the basic things to contribute, or to learn, being a complete victim to life, and pushing his family away. That's how I saw what Alex was doing. The next question is how I see what I am doing. All of this is coming from my journal I wrote at the Monastery in 2019. I saw that I was protecting my family, helping Alex grow up and face the real world, standing up for myself, not taking his abuse, teaching him how to be a good adult, trying to build a connection with him, paying for everything, and providing for him. The third question is how does the other person, in this case, Alex, see what I am doing? So again, I put myself in his shoes. How does he see what I am doing? Alex saw me as trying to control him, make him into me, not listening to him, trying to force a relationship and a life view that he doesn't want, wielding my money as a weapon, as a stick to get him under control, not giving him space or room to grow, suffocating him. Yikes! That's right. He feels like I am suffocating him with my nonstop pressure. The fourth question is, how does the other person, in this case, Alex, see what he is doing? Again, I put myself in his situation and asked how he saw what he was doing. He's trying to be a normal teenager and figure life out, trying to become his own man. He feels he is protecting himself from a formerly angry dad and from a relationship that he feels I might throw away again, as he felt I did when I sent him out to the equine therapy ranch. This was very enlightening for me to see this collusion diagram and to feel how *he* felt. It helped move my heart from being in correction mode to understanding and love.

This reminds me of another tool, from *The Anatomy of Peace*, that we can use to transform our hearts from war to peace. It is especially effective for parents, as we spend so much time correcting our children. We want them to be a certain way. And that almost always starts with correcting what's gone wrong instead of helping things go right. This is called the Relational Leadership Pyramid, or the pyramid of change. I spent most of my time with my children at the very top of the pyramid, trying to get them to change, correcting them. And most of the time, that didn't work. And yet, I still would stick with that. I would stick with trying to correct them, and then it would escalate and sometimes get quite heated. When correcting doesn't work, I must consider the fact that they might not know what they are doing is wrong. I need to slow down, drop to the next level, and teach them what to do. And if that doesn't work, which in my case, it didn't, then I need to listen to them. I need to see where they're coming from. I need to work on my relationship with them.

And if I can't even build a relationship directly with them, I need to work on my relationship with people who have an influence on them. With Alex, our relationship was so broken, I couldn't even work on the relationship with him. I needed to work on my relationships with people around him, with his mom, his grandparents, his siblings, and his friends, and that eventually invited him into the possibility of being back in a relationship with me. And if that still doesn't work, if I still cannot connect with him, then I really need to look at my own way of being. Is my heart at peace, or is my heart at war? Am I approaching him as a human being or an object? I need to look at my own heart. That is by far the biggest area in the pyramid because it also has the biggest effect. If our own heart isn't right, nothing else works.

Most of my work has been on my own heart, my own way of being, as you heard earlier. This pyramid is a great tool to reflect on any time we're working on a relationship with somebody that we love, especially someone that we're in a leadership position over or have authority over. We may be trying to teach or trying to correct when we need to be looking at our own hearts. Is it at peace where we're seeing others as human beings and we're letting go of the outcome? Or is it at war where we're controlling and trying to make it a certain way and not seeing others fully as human beings, as we are?

I'll share one story about this that may relate to some of you parents out there as well. Alex was about 12, and we had friends over with their kids who were younger than Alex. He would become dysregulated very easily. That's what reactive attachment disorder (RAD) does. The child sees everything as life or death and goes into fight or flight mode, dysregulation, at what seems completely inconsequential to someone without RAD. When he became dysregulated, he would start cussing. My first reaction was not, "Oh man, Alex is struggling, and I need help to calm down and take care of him." My first reaction was, "What will this other family think? Their young kids are around my 12-year-old kid, who's dropping a bunch of F-bombs? They will think I am a bad father." Looking back on that, after I had this realization in 2019, it was another point of evidence that I was more concerned about how I was seen by them than having consideration for Alex. At that time, I did not see him as a human being, but as an object, an accessory to me, to my life.

So how do you see others as human beings, not objects, in the present moment? Let me share one more tool from *The Anatomy of Peace*, and this is a very subtle thing. Every time we interact with a loved one or any human being, we have a sense of what is the right thing to do. It's a small nudge, a small voice that says, "Do this, not that," "Put away your daughter's dishes," or "Stop to see how your teammate is doing," or "Get up and take care of the crying baby so your partner can sleep." We have this small sense of the right thing to do. If we follow that sense, we are seeing them as human beings. And our hearts will be at peace. And if we don't follow that sense, what's the first thing that we do? We justify it to ourselves. If I have the thought, "You know, I should go check on my daughter and see how she's doing with this heavy homework project." And I don't do that, the first thing that I do when I ignore that sense is to justify it to myself. I reason, "Well, I've got this big work project I'm really busy with, and she's really smart and she doesn't need my help. My project is more important than her homework." That starts the separation. I see her not as fully human as I see myself. And subtly, I'm making my work project more important than my connection with her and making myself, therefore, a little bit more important than her in my own mind. So that's a great way to check and to catch yourself in the moment. If you follow your senses, you see them as human. If not, just a little less than. Follow that sense!

Summary and Actions:

Love wins. Developing love for God, for yourself, and for others is the most important job we have. Use gratitude to connect with your love of God, use grace and the "I love myself" process, meditation, and questions, to grow in your love for self. Finally, love others. Check in and see if you are seeing them as human beings or as objects. Use the tools from the book, *The Anatomy of Peace*, and the realizations from *Bonds that Make Us Free*, to understand if you are seeing others as human beings or as objects. Follow your senses in your interactions with others, especially loved ones. Consider the power of forgiveness, both in granting it to others and seeking it for yourself, as a bridge to understanding and compassion. Reflect on how forgiveness can open the door to viewing everyone around you, particularly those closest to you, through a lens of empathy and humanity, rather than judgment or ownership. This act of forgiveness is a crucial step in transforming relationships from conflict to connection, guiding your journey toward a heart at peace with love as its compass. Make the relationship a priority over being right, being more important, or having respect. What relationships are working well in your life? Which ones are not? Are you treating everyone as a human being? What sense about how to behave in your key relationships have you not followed that you will follow now? Reflect on these questions. Use these tools. They will move your heart from anger and turmoil to a heart at peace, as I did with my transformation in the desert and the years that followed.

Chapter 9:
Gratitude Transforms Your Life

"Gratitude can transform any situation. It alters your vibration, moving you from negative energy to positive. It's the quickest, easiest, most powerful way to effect change in your life – this I know for sure."

~ Oprah Winfrey

First, what is gratitude? It is an appreciation of what we already experience in our lives, right here and now. Appreciating something literally means adding value to it. We add value to the moments and experiences by giving them our attention and positive energy. It is thankfulness. If we have wonderful things and experiences but are not grateful for them, we might as well not have them. They bring no joy or happiness.

Which comes first: are we grateful because we are happy, or are we happy because we are grateful? For most of my life, I thought it was the former. When I was happy, I would be grateful for whatever had happened to make me happy. The issue with this is that I am looking for something external, something I don't control, to make me happy. In his TED Talk, David Steindl-Rast changed my perspective.

https://www.ted.com/talks/david_steindl_rast_want_to_be _happy_be_grateful?language=en

He makes the case that we are happy when we are grateful. And what triggers gratitude is a gift of high value, freely given with no strings attached. Just waking up another day is exactly such a gift. Nothing has a higher value than life, and it is given to us freely to do with what we will. Just tapping into this, really feeling it, makes me smile. I have a gift of immense value that I am unwrapping today. I start each day with this realization. I list and journal 5 items that I am grateful for in my life, with a focus on the previous day. But it can be anything that comes into my heart at that moment, and I feel grateful or thankful for it. It often is a hug from a family member the previous day, the beautiful sunrise going on right now, or the hot cup of tea I am holding, and the warmth that it brings. It is often also for my wife or other loved ones. And it often includes my health and fitness, from being able to see, to the deep breath I just took, to running, and being able to run and hike. There is so much to be grateful for just in the moment, the gift of each day. I also end each day by discussing with my wife what we are each grateful for from the day. This anchors gratitude on both ends of my day.

After years of practicing gratitude in this way, my life is much happier in two ways. In the short term, my perspective changes each time I focus on what I am grateful for, and that makes me happier in the moment. Secondly, the cumulative effect of that over the last few years shows in the "facts of my life," not just in my perspective. The most obvious effect is on the relationships with my immediate family and how that, in turn, affects the total environment of my life. This was on full display yesterday as we prepared Thanksgiving dinner for 11 at our home. Years ago, hosting was quite stressful. First, I was stressed and wanted everything to be perfect. This energy negatively affected others. My relationships with my kids were not nearly as good as today, so I spent a lot of time chasing them to help and then feeling bad if they didn't. The gratitude I have been practicing the last few years has made me much easier going, dramatically improving the relationships with my children, so it is fun for them to work together with us now.

This was on full display during Thanksgiving yesterday, and for that, I am truly grateful. Our day was perfectly imperfect and so much fun.

Especially in America, we focus so much on what we want to accomplish, to achieve. We want straight A's in school, and then to get into the best college and have a great career so we can be CEO and make a lot of money and buy a great house, be important, etc. Or do we want to be a social media influencer and see many out there with millions of followers when we only have a few? We feel that gap between what we want and what we have, and we feel bad. We feel less than. And then we feel we should work harder to close that gap, and we play less, work more, obsess more, and even deprive ourselves of sleep to study or work. Then our mood tanks, we are mean to those around us, and we start to damage our relationships with those we love most. This is all because we are focusing on the gap, on what we don't have or have not accomplished compared to someone else. And that gap will *always* be there, no matter how much we do or achieve. If we have 1M followers, there is someone with more. If we have $100M, there is someone with $1B. The gap will never go away, so it is a doom spiral. How do we stop this? We appreciate what we already have and experience today, no matter what it is. The Bible tells us in 1 Thessalonians 5:18 to "Give thanks for everything." That is a high standard, but that is the intention: to always be focused on the good in our lives, what we do appreciate. Even in a very bad situation, there are things to be grateful for. If you get dumped by a friend, you can be grateful for other friends to grieve with and for the good experiences you had with that friend while they lasted. If you get injured, you can be grateful for the use of that foot most of the time, how wonderful it is to walk without crutches, and how good it is to have family and friends to help you recover. So, the other way to close that gap is to want what you have, to appreciate that. That one is much easier to do, and you feel better immediately. There is nothing that improves my mood faster than being truly grateful.

Summary and Actions:

Gratitude may be the most powerful tool we have to improve our life experience immediately. It is also completely in our control to use it or not. How do I be grateful? Practice! There are so many ways, from apps to journals, and I recommend you start simply by writing down or speaking five things you are grateful for first thing every morning and last thing at night. Sharing it with a partner magnifies it and strengthens your relationship with them as well. Another great way is to set your phone or watch timer to vibrate every hour to remind you to be grateful for one thing right then. Before we go on, stop, breathe deeply, and notice five things you are grateful for right now. Write them down here.

Gratitude List:

1. _____

2. _____

3. _____

4. _____

5. _____

Make sure you have written all five. One more assignment: What is going to be your gratitude practice? Start small, but start, and attach it to something else you do every day. Maybe it is to say one thing you are grateful for as you start to eat breakfast.

My Gratitude Practice is...

Do it each day. Be grateful for the wonderful gift of today and every day. Be grateful and see how that immediately improves how you feel and slowly improves your entire life.

Chapter 10:
Respect Is Always in Fashion

"Everyone should be respected as an individual, but no one idolized."

~ Albert Einstein

Just as you are worthy and deserving of respect just by being a human being, just by being a child of God, so is every other human being. Everyone is doing the best they know and deserves that same basic human dignity and respect from you. What does respect look like? It starts with a state of mind about that person that matches their human dignity. I say to myself, "You are a divine being," to each person I encounter. Recognizing the sacred within them, their spark of divinity automatically puts me in a respectful mood toward them.

It is also very important to see what respect is not. Dr. John M. Gottman, the world's leading expert on emotional intelligence, puts it best. He can accurately predict whether a couple will get divorced or not after only a few minutes of watching their interactions. The two biggest contributors are contempt and disgust. Contempt is where people show signs of contempt toward each other by rolling their eyes and exasperating sighs. Disgust is where he looks for facial expressions showing disgust: fast exhales with the chin jutting down, or the shaking of the head with a look of disgust. These are NOT respect. These are the ways you treat people when you are disrespectful. Treating people that way will ensure that you destroy the relationship and turn them off from helping you.

Being respectful also does not mean condoning bad behavior or letting them do things that hurt you. In fact, the opposite is true. If you really respect someone, you will respect them enough, care about them enough, to tell them the truth even if it is uncomfortable for you. If someone continually engages me in hurtful, contemptuous, disrespectful behavior, I must respect *myself* enough to take a stand that I am not going to put up with it anymore. It is very uncomfortable for me, but it is my willingness to be uncomfortable, to take a stand, that will help reach a breakthrough in the relationship. I can remember a time with one of my young children, after having a very tough discussion about what is OK and what is not OK, we had one of the best, most respectful, connected, value-adding conversations we have ever had. After I respected myself enough to take a stand, they respected me enough to stop and listen, and we both got to see and talk about the way we wanted our relationship to be. As discussed earlier in this book, the first step of getting what you want is to identify it. That night, we both got clear on what it was we wanted in our relationship and started to go there. It all started with respecting each other.

Yesterday on the news, I saw a young ESPN reporter who was ruining her career by treating a parking attendant with disrespect. She had the whole world at her feet. She is young, beautiful, articulate, and rising fast in the ranks. But she has been suspended for berating and cussing at a parking attendant in a garage that had towed her car. It is OK to be frustrated and to be upset, but never ok to berate or belittle or cuss and put down another human being. That will always end badly for you. Always. It may look like you have won the battle, but you will lose the war.

I know there is a tendency to look down on those who we feel do work that is less important than ours. Alex, this is just like you when you were disrespectful to our housekeeper, Qin Ayi, in China. You thought she was below you, and you treated her with contempt. But how good did she make you feel when you came home to a clean house? That is a gift, a real gift, my son. And for that gift, she deserves your honor and respect. And I later saw that come out in you, even as you would try to scare her, but it was a connection and in an honoring way that you both loved. She would freak out and then smile and walk off and say, "That ALEX!" and you would smile a loving smile. That is showing love and respect. When you threw stuff on the floor and said, "It doesn't matter, Qin will clean it up" with contempt, that was wrong, and that is why you lost her cleaning your room and had to do it yourself. Treating people with respect will always help you get what you want, and treating people with disrespect will always distance you from what you want.

Here is another example. This morning, when I was checking in at the Nashville airport on my way to Shanghai, there was a very rude young man demanding the customer service reps help him find his phone that he had left on the parking bus. He was being very disrespectful and really upset the customer service reps. Finally, they told him to go downstairs and talk to the customer service office. His plane was about to depart, and I am sure he really wanted to get on that plane, but his disrespectful behavior kept him from getting what he wanted. The agent at the desk told me that if he had only been respectful, we would have called the parking company for him and asked that they deliver his phone at once, but since he was so disrespectful, we don't even want to help him.

Here is one final example. When I was Director of the GM Europe business unit in Germany, I had a very important customer out with me to dinner. I thought highly of this person, and they were very important to our business. We were in a nice restaurant, and the service was a little slow. This person berated the server, treating them completely disrespectfully, just yelling and belittling them. I lost all respect for this person, and shortly thereafter, they lost their job, and I have not talked with them since. If they were a kind and respectful person, I would have made an effort to help them, but when they were so disrespectful to a person that they felt could do them no harm, they became a much smaller person in my eyes, and I had no desire to help them in future hardships. How we treat those who can't do anything for us tells us much more about ourselves than it does about them.

That is a lot about disrespect, so what does respect look like? It is truly valuing the other person. Be kind, compassionate, empathetic, caring, courageous, engaging, and come from your heart. In a word, love. It is giving them your full attention when you are engaged with them, not looking at your phone or interrupting. The greatest gift we can give another human being is the purity of our attention. To really see them. Everyone wants to be seen and talked to, and no one wants to be watched or talked about. Use your manners, see the divinity in them. Be kind. Follow the Golden Rule: treat others as you want to be treated.

Summary and Actions:

All human beings deserve dignity and respect just for being human beings, just like you deserve their respect just for being a human being. When you show that respect to all people, you will feel good about yourself, being the kind of person God intends for you to be. Engage with others as you would want them to engage with you. You will also get much more of what you want in life. When you forget yourself and treat others with disrespect, you will not get what you want, and you will feel bad about yourself. For that reason, respect is ALWAYS in fashion and always the right thing. When you treat others with respect, your life will be much better, and you will feel good. Incorporate small acts of kindness into your daily routine as tangible expressions of respect. These gestures, though seemingly minor, can profoundly impact the well-being of both you and those around you, reinforcing the essence of human dignity in every encounter. One of the universal and consistent ways to show respect is with good manners, which we talk about in the next chapter.

Chapter 11:
Manners are the Oil in the Gears of Life

"Good manners will open doors that the best education cannot. "

~ Justice Clarence Thomas, U.S. Supreme Court

Do you ever wonder why Mom and I tell you constantly to use your manners? I am sure it gets annoying after a while. But there is a very good reason for it. Let me ask you this. How do you feel when one of your siblings comes and grabs one of your things without asking? I see the results. You grab it back, hit each other, and call names, or come running to one of us, complaining loudly. How would you feel if one of your siblings came up to you and said, "Can I please play with your phone for 30 minutes because my phone is dead and is charging, and I really want to play Crossy Road? You are on the Xbox right now anyway, and if you want something else, you can use my DS during that time. I will be very careful with it, and I will only play Crossy Road and then give it back to you in 30 minutes. Is that ok?" How would you feel? You may still not want to let them, but you feel MUCH better about it. You are not angry. Now, let's change roles.

Now you are the one who asks. When you grab your siblings' things and they get angry, what does it accomplish? Do you actually get to play with the toys you grab? More often than not it results in not-so-fun consequences and you

74

don't get the toy either. When you ask with good manners, respect, and explanation, what happens? Are you more likely to get what you want? The answer is always YES! By being respectful and using basic manners, you are always more likely to get what you want.

If you are reading a book and it is past your bedtime, and I come to you and say, "Alex, it is past your bedtime. Please turn the lights off now." Does this feel better than if I come in and turn off the lights? Of course, it does. If you say "No!" in a snotty tone, how likely do you think it is that I let you keep the lights on? If you stop, look me in the eye, and while holding up the book, you say, "Daddy, I only have this much left until the end of the chapter. It is VERY interesting right now, and it will only take me two minutes to finish. Can I please finish the chapter and then turn out the lights?" How do you think I will react? There is a 90% chance I will let you finish the chapter just because of the way you asked, because you used good manners.

What are manners? Manners are the words, tone, facial expressions, and body language you use when you interact with others. Good manners are those actions taken when you do it with good cheer and respect, and dignity for the other person. Putting it very simply, it is how you treat the other person so they will feel good about your interaction. You treat them kindly and compassionately. Here are the basics. First, always address the person by name or title and look them in the eyes when trying to get their attention. If you are interrupting, wait a minute for them to see you first and see if they will just acknowledge you. If they don't and it can wait, come back another time. If it is VERY urgent, say, "Please excuse the interruption, and I need to talk to you as soon as you can." Then wait for them to give you their attention. If you approach a parent or a boss while they are talking with someone else, wait a minute (really a minute, not 3 seconds!) More than likely, she will say, "Hi Kayli, is it urgent or can it wait a minute as I am talking to Sawyer here?" You would answer, speaking clearly and looking her in the eyes, "Thanks, Mom, it is urgent and will only take one minute, and you can continue your conversation with Sawyer. Mira is at the door and wants to know if I can come over to play. I would like to. Can I go with her, please? What time do I need to be home?"

"Six," Mom replies.

"Thanks very much and sorry for the interruption." You conclude.

If she doesn't give you her attention after one minute, and 60 long seconds, then speak in a clear, respectful voice and say, "I am sorry to interrupt, but I need your attention for just 30 seconds as soon as you can, please." and take it from there.

Second, always answer kindly when someone is talking to you. If you are reading or watching TV and someone approaches, hit the pause button, or put the book down and give them your attention. Look up with a smile and say pleasantly, "Hi, do you want something?" If you hear Mom or Dad calling you, please answer at once so that we know if you heard us or not.

Third, use "please" and "thank you." It seems so trite and trivial today, but it is just as important and as in-fashion as ever. Why is it important? So that you can be the kind of person you want to be (kind and respectful) and so that you have a better chance of getting what you want. At the table, "Sawyer, would you please pass me the salt?" is going to leave everyone feeling good—and much more likely to get you the salt—than "Give me the salt!" With "Give me the salt!" no one will know whom you are addressing, and no one will feel like obliging you. Then, when you receive the salt, say, "Thank you, Sawyer." And better yet, say it with a smile, which makes both of you feel good. Sawyer returns the smile and eye contact and says genuinely, "You are welcome."

Underlying all manners is basic respect and empathy for others. It is the essence of the Golden Rule, which tells us to treat others the way we would want to be treated. How would you want to be spoken to? Address them like that. How would you want people to react to you when you speak to them? React that way. Be aware of those around you and tune into what is going on with them. Feel what they are feeling. That is empathy. Hold the door for the mom pushing a stroller into the grocery store. If there are two of you approaching an entrance at the same time, defer to the other with a smile and a wave of the hand.

And this is even more important outside the home than inside. When you talk to your teachers, good manners will get you much farther than not. If you follow the same steps above and talk to your teachers with respect, good eye contact, and "please and thank you," you are much more likely to get what you want. If you need help with a project and you say, "Give me help!" you will not get it, especially if you do it with a snotty tone. If you say, "Mrs. Craig, I don't understand problem three of the homework I did last night. Am I supposed to multiply or add the numbers?" She will help you. If you disrespect a teacher by talking when they are speaking, not giving them your attention, rolling your eyes, not holding eye contact when they are talking to you, or not using "please" and "thank you," they will label you as disrespectful and, without even knowing it, they will grade you a little harder and they will never bend the rules for you. On the other hand, if you have good manners, they will label you as respectful and a good student and give you the benefit of the doubt on grading and may bend the rules for you.

It is the same in your professional life. The last thing your boss will tolerate is bad manners and disrespect. Yes, results count, and if your boss doesn't like you because of your lack of manners, you will not get the promotion to the next position where you can make bigger results. Good manners with your colleagues will get their goodwill and support, which is essential to be successful in today's workplace. If you are an independent professional, say a teacher or lawyer, having good manners with your clients or students will make you much more effective and successful, helping them much more and bringing you more rewards in your career.

Finally, good manners are most important in personal

relationships, especially romantic ones. You will never attract or keep a wonderful spouse without having good manners, empathy, and respect. It is easy to take those we love the most for granted, so it is extra important to be kind and respectful, shown in good manners, to our loved ones.

In all situations in life, family, school, work, travel, sports, and romantic relationships, the actions to be successful and happy happen with and through people. These people are like gears in a transmission, going in and out of contact with each other many times. They all must work together to get what they want in life. When one turns, it turns the other and creates the results. You can say manners have no value, as they are not the gears, and the transmission turns just fine with just the gears. And that is true, but only for a short time. If you run the transmission fast or hard, even just for a few minutes without oil, the transmission will get very hot and lock up, and if pushed a little harder, it will be completely destroyed. It is the same with manners. If you don't have them, things may work OK in the short term, especially if you are in a position of power or if there is no pressure, but after a while or added pressure, all the relationships will get hot and lock up, and if not attended to, they will be completely destroyed, and you will be alone. So, keep the oil in the transmission, and the manners in your interactions; his will keep your life running much more smoothly over the long term, and you will enjoy it much more too.

Conclusion:

Manners are like oil in the gears of life. Treat everyone

with kindness and dignity in every interaction. Take a minute now to look back at the last week and see where you have good manners and where they need to improve. Write down a few concrete examples. Now see how you can apply what you did well to those situations where you didn't do as well. Will you add kindness, a smile, eye contact, genuine interest in the other person, or patience? Make a note of it and mostly be tuned into the people and situations around you, and show respect and empathy, and you will make others happier, feel better about yourself, and get more of what you want from life.

Chapter 12:
Character: Have It! Don't Be One

"Human greatness does not lie in wealth or power, but in character and goodness."

~ Anne Frank, the world's most widely known diarist, and a Jewish victim of the Holocaust.

Do you ever have times when you really don't feel like doing something you have committed to doing? Say homework? Or cleaning up your room? Or applying for that new job? Or writing that book? Do you ever just not want to do it and keep putting it off until the last minute or not do it at all? I know the answer is yes because I do, too. I have not felt like writing in this book for the last few years, and I haven't done it. I still don't feel like writing this morning, but I am doing it anyway. That is character.

Character is doing what you said you would do long after the mood in which you said it has left you. Since I was inspired to and committed to writing this book to share my main life learnings with you, then good character means I must do it. I must follow through even though many mornings I am not in that mood, or I am "too busy." It means doing the homework during your homework time, since that is when you said you would do it when you were inspired to get straight A's this term, even though you would much rather jump on the trampoline or have screen time right now. It means that I lace up my running shoes and head out into the cold, dark morning because that is what is on my training plan today, even if I would much rather sleep in. It means that I under promise and overdeliver in my career. It drives reflection and discipline on both ends. First, I am much more careful about what I choose to commit to. I reflect on both why I want to do it and on when it is reasonable to get it done BEFORE I commit to it. And on the back end, I follow through on what I said I was going to do and keep other affected people appraised of the status. It doesn't mean I am never late, but I always let the other party know as soon as I know I will be late, to maintain my integrity.

That to me is the real meaning of having character. And it applies almost everywhere. You become a man or woman of your word by developing your character. It is a life-long journey, just like exercising, breathing, or eating. You will always be making mistakes and always keep growing. You can never get to a point where you say, "My character is developed, so I can take a day off from doing what I said I was going to do. You know I have been developing my character for 4,000 days straight. I am going to stop now. A few days won't matter." That would be like taking a day or even an hour off from breathing. You could say, "I have been breathing for 175,200 hours straight. I deserve a break and will take just one hour off." You would be dead in that one hour. Of course, it is not so quick with some other things, but the bottom line is that you must keep doing what you said you would, and you must keep integrity with yourself and those around you if you want to develop your character. There is no in-between; you are either building it or destroying it. For example, being married to your mom, I have made a promise to keep myself only to her for romantic love for the rest of her life. If I chose to take just one day off from that, it would destroy my character and our relationship. This may seem unfair, as I have had 8,030 days of keeping my word. Just one shouldn't matter, right? But it does. We all make mistakes. We must clean them up when we do and start building our good character again. It is important to always have character and not be one.

You don't want to be a character in this sense. Don't be the guy that others describe as "He or she is such a character!" That usually means you are not doing what you have said you would do, that you have not been building your character, but being one. You are being disrespectful or at least inappropriate to the situation. Often this is being loud or causing disruption in class or in the family. It is often inappropriately seeking attention and validation that can come from not knowing that you are worthy just as you are. It is any time we are inappropriate to the situation, being driven by our impulses and fears instead of love and compassion. Whatever the cause, don't be a character— unless you are in a play or movie. :-)

Keep your word to yourself and others, especially when you don't feel like it, and you will have character instead of being one. Every time you keep your word, you are building your character. You are strengthening yourself, your will, and your discipline. As you get stronger in this way, you will be able to do more of the things you want to in all areas of your life, meaning your life is working. The degree to which you keep your word is the degree to which your life works.

On the other hand, have you had times when your life is not working so well? This could be when you get a failing grade at school or when you are super stressed working on a huge assignment at the last minute. What happened there? Go ahead, answer it for yourself. And if you say, I don't know, I will tell you. You didn't keep your word. There were many times along the way when you said you would do your homework that night or work on the project for 2 hours each Saturday for 5 weeks. But instead of keeping your word, you played video games, or Legos, or read. Then you said you would make up for it tomorrow and do 4 hours then. But then there was church, and your friends came over to play, and we had a family fun time, all of which are good things. And you said to yourself, you would do it after dinner, but then you played with Dudley, bounced on the trampoline, got tired, and suddenly it was bedtime. After you put enough of those days together of not keeping your word, you are sitting there on the last night, very stressed, trying to get your project done or cramming for the exam. And if you don't keep your word and give up, you will get a failing grade.

On the flip side, when you keep your word and do your homework each day, you get good grades. You don't feel stressed and overwhelmed, and your school life is working. By keeping your word to yourself and your teacher by doing the assignments each day as they are due, you have a great experience as well. Alex, I think of your recent project on the history of video games. You worked on that steadily over the term and in the end had time to make a very creative scrapbook and presentation, as well as having many physical examples. You kept your word and delivered a great project, and I think you even had a good time doing it.

Your life is working there! Sawyer, I saw the same with your Solar System project last week. You worked on it steadily and came up with a very creative and super cool presentation in Prezi. Keeping your word to yourself each day makes your life work.

Another good example is your health. This is one I struggle with a lot, too. I say, "I will not eat carbs this week," and then if I don't eat them, keeping my word, my life works. I lose weight and feel great. And the battle is won or lost in the little conversation we have in our heads. If I give in to that voice that says, "It is OK. Just one little brownie. Just one piece of Easter cake. I mean, after all, Oma made it for us, so it would be rude not to eat it. Come on, you have been so good. You have been fasting for the last week. One little treat won't hurt anything. You can eat some extra salad and run a little extra...tomorrow." If we give in to that voice, we will not keep our word, and we will gain weight. We need to make a stronger voice that focuses on what we want by keeping our word. We need to have a voice that says, "Better out than in. I want to be able to do the epic hike at Philmont or run the sub-4-hour marathon. To do that, I need to make my target weight, and eating this piece of cake or candy will not support me with that goal, so I will not eat it. I want to feed my body good stuff that makes me feel good, so I will eat some carrots and hummus for a snack instead." When we listen to that voice, we make it stronger, and by doing so, we keep our word more often. And the more we keep our word, the more our life works.

Alex, for you, it could be doing your foot exercises each

day. When you keep that word to yourself, your feet don't hurt, and you can run and jump on the trampoline and do flips without any pain. Your life is working in that area. If you don't do them, you are very limited in what you can do, and you complain and hurt all the time, and your life is not working. Another one for you could be having good nutrition each day. When you eat healthy fats and proteins, your brain functions much better, and you remember to turn in your assignments and bring your science book home with you. When you don't keep your word to me and yourself about having good brain nutrition and drink soda and eat unhealthy fats (burgers and fries or ribs), you forget things and get stressed and overwhelmed very quickly.

Kayli, what is an example for you? Maybe when you keep your word to me and Mom by staying in eyesight when playing outside with your friends, you get to have a good time and have play dates whenever you want. When you don't keep your word there, you can't have play dates for a month, and that friend area of your life is not working. Also in school, if you keep your word by following the character and class rules, you are liked by the teacher and your friends. And when you don't keep that word, you are stressed, feel targeted by the teacher, and your school life is not working so well, and we have to all meet together with the counselor.

We all have areas of our lives where we are keeping our word to a higher degree, and our lives are working better because of it. A good example is my work with Autoliv. I keep my word, and it is working very well. Kayli, you can see it with your gymnastics and your grades. You practice gymnastics all the time, and you keep your word on your homework, even when you don't feel like it, and it shows with straight A's last semester. Alex, you can see it with your reading, your Legos, and your backflips. Sawyer, you can see it very clearly with your friendships and your schoolwork. The secret is to take the areas where you keep your word and apply those to the areas where it is not. Sawyer, I think you would always keep your word to your friends. Well, maybe have one of them help you with your eating. Alex, you never skip a day at home doing backflips on the trampoline. So, commit yourself to doing your foot exercises before your flips. Same with homework, keep your word by ensuring that you have your homework done before reading or playing video games. Kayli, you would never think of missing gymnastics class, so have that same commitment to your word with your behavior with your friends. When you do these things, your life will work great, and you will have more fun and more options as you go along.

A good measure of this is the following poem. He wrote it to himself, but please take it to include everyone, not just him. And "pelf" is not a typo for self, but his version of who you are in total. It is also about how to check in with yourself and make sure you are loving yourself, and to ensure you are developing your character, not being one.

The Guy in the Glass:

When you get what you want in your struggle for pelf,
And the world makes you King for a day,

87

Chapter 12: Character: Have it! Don't be One

Then go to the mirror and look at yourself,
And see what that guy has to say.
For it isn't your Father, or Mother, or Wife,
Whose judgment upon you must pass.
The feller whose verdict counts most in your life
Is the guy staring back from the glass.
He's the feller to please, never mind all the rest,
For he's with you clear up to the end,
And you've passed your most dangerous, difficult test
If the guy in the glass is your friend.
You may be like Jack Horner and "chisel" a plum,
And think you're a wonderful guy,
But the man in the glass says you're only a bum
If you can't look him straight in the eye.
You can fool the whole world down the pathway of
years,
And get pats on the back as you pass,
But your final reward will be heartaches and tears
If you've cheated the guy in the glass.
Dale Wimbrow 1895-1954

*Permission for the reproduction of "The Guy in the Glass" was very kindly granted to me by the family of Dale Wimbrow. Please contact the Wimbrow family before reproducing the poem. This is one of the most misquoted and misrepresented writings that I know of - by gaining proper permission from the Wimbrow family, we can finally show Dale the gratitude and respect that he rightfully deserves.

I love this poem. It reminds me that the only one who can

truly judge if you have character is you. Stay true to yourself, no matter what, and you will always be friends with the guy or gal in the glass, and by that, you will know you have character.

Summary and Actions:

I love the saying from Britain's first female Prime Minister, Margaret Thatcher. She said, "Be careful what you think, as it creates what you say. Be careful what you say, as it creates what you do. Be careful what you do, as it creates your character. And be careful with your character, as it creates your destiny!" This is so true. If you want a great destiny and an amazing life, build a great character by keeping your word to yourself and others, instead of being a character that others laugh at. How do we build good character? Be thoughtful about what commitments you make. Then keep your word to yourself and others, and clean it up right away when you make mistakes. You will have good character instead of being one.

Chapter 13:
Teamwork Wins!

"It is not finance, not strategy, not intelligence, but teamwork that remains the ultimate competitive advantage both because it is so powerful and so rare."

~ Patrick Lencioni

I love this quote. It is so true. But what is teamwork? Teamwork is a group of people who choose to work or play together toward a common goal that they all agree is important, and they don't care who gets the credit. There is no "I" in "team," literally and figuratively. It is only about how to best accomplish the *common* goal. And working together always creates better results. It is possible you are the smartest and most knowledgeable about the team goal, and even so, the input of the other members of the team will make the results better than if you did it alone.

A great example is this story from Robyn Benincasa, who is the world's best female adventure racer. She and her team take on the toughest multi-day endurance races and Eco-challenges in the world and win more than any others. And these challenges would be impossible to do alone. How do they win? By being a real team! She talks about seeing more fit individuals, like a whole team of Navy Seals, where each one is fitter than anyone on her team, but they only last one day on the course because they don't have teamwork. They fight with each other and are more concerned with looking good individually and being right and what is "fair" than what the team needs to win. Her teams are completely free of this. For her teams to work, it is critical that everyone gets what they need when they need it, not "what is fair." In one race, they were running/hiking through 50 miles of outback virgin jungle in Australia. They had to carry everything they needed for the full week with them, so they all had 50 lb. backpacks. When she was 10 miles into the hike, she was very tired but didn't want to burden her other teammates, so she kept going. One of the big, strong guys saw she was suffering and took her pack from her, and the 5 men on the team took turns carrying it for the next 39 miles. They were in first place as they were coming into the next checkpoint, which was full of people and TV cameras. Without saying anything, her teammates handed her pack back to her before they came into view, so it would seem she was carrying it the whole time. There are two great lessons here. The first and obvious one is that her strong teammates had no ego. They didn't complain about carrying her pack together with their 50-pounder for most of the trip, and they didn't even want credit from the TV crews for doing it. They were just doing what was needed for the good of the team. The second one was less obvious. Later that night, her teammates gave Robyn a hard time, saying, "Why didn't you ask for help earlier?" And she said she didn't want to burden the team. She wanted to carry her own weight. She didn't want to let the team down by not doing her share. She wanted it to be fair. The big guy who first took her pack was quite wise. He said one of the most important things anyone can do to be a good teammate is to ask for help when they need it and to graciously accept it when offered. He scolded her, "Robyn, if you had kept your pack on and then hit the wall, the whole team would have suffered, and we would have lost. I can carry your pack just fine, but I can't carry you!" It is not about being "fair," but about each team member getting what they need and giving what they can so that the team has the best chance of success. It is really important to ask for help when you first need it, so you don't bring the whole team down. And if you are offered help, graciously accept. It is a gift to the one offering the help. This applies just as well to team projects at school or work. If you are struggling with your part of the project, don't hide it, as it will bring down the whole team's goal. Ask for help so the team still has a chance to be successful. And if someone sees you dropping behind or not getting done what is needed and offers to help, accept the help graciously. Think about it. If Mom is really struggling to carry in 6 bags of groceries at once and you offer to help her, and she says, "No! I can get it myself!" How does that feel, to be rejected? If she had said, "Oh, thank you, that is a big help," you would feel great, and she would have given you a gift by accepting your help. If you see a teammate struggling on their part and you offer to help them, and they react defensively, how does that feel to you? Not good. Ask for help when you need it. Offer help when you see the need.

What is your best experience of teamwork? Was it your sports team? A group project at school? Working together to achieve a project in the family? To readers who are not my children, was it a great work project? Or working on the farm? Stop reading for a minute, close your eyes, and remember your best team experience. Reflect on it. What made it great? What did you like about it? What made it memorable? Write those two or three things down. Were you the leader or a team member? What behaviors from the leader or other members made it fun and effective? What did you do to contribute to the feeling of a team? To the fun? To the success?

One of my best experiences with teamwork was getting the hay in before the rain when I was 12 years old. We were living on a 50-acre commune/homestead with cows, chickens, and crops, but we didn't have any tractors. We did everything by hand. We scythed the hay (or walked behind the cycle bar). Then we would turn the hay by hand with a pitchfork, and then after a few days of drying in the sun, we would pick it up with those same pitchforks, load it in a hand cart, and pull it to the barn. There, we would carefully layer the hay into a haystack that would be 8-10 feet high at the end of the summer to feed the cows through the winter. The most important thing about making hay is that it dries out without ever getting rained on. If it doesn't get dry enough, it can get hot and burn the barn down as it ferments, and if it gets any rain on it, it becomes a waste and can't be fed to the animals. It becomes mushroom hay. The stakes are high! This time, the hay had just gotten dry enough to put up, and there were big storm clouds on the horizon. The rain was coming! And if it got there before we got the hay in, it would be a total loss, and we might not have enough to feed our cows through the long Pennsylvania winter. Here we were, about 10 children from 10-15 years old and a couple of parents. We saw the clouds and knew we must get this hay into the barn before the rain. Everyone knew this, and then something magical happened. We didn't worry about who worked harder than whom, what job we had, or what was fair. We all jumped in and worked like crazy, loading the hay in the cart, running it to the barn a few hundred yards away, forking it over the haystack, and running back out to do it again. We had several carts and were all working like crazy. It was so much fun! When someone just ran the cart to the barn, they would collapse on the ground to catch their breath while someone else unloaded. When I got tired of pulling the cart, I asked for help, and two boys jumped in and started pushing from behind. No one complained, and everyone pitched in and worked hard TOGETHER. Even though we worked extremely hard, it was also so much fun. It was such a bonding experience. We got the last cart to the barn just as the rain started to pour down! That is my favorite team experience, and it was this teamwork that fed the cows that winter.

This is just as true at work, even if it is more complicated, because most work teams don't have the foundation of trust we have in our family. The team or the whole company will fail if one of the members fails badly enough, so not asking for help when you need it can be the worst thing you can do for the success of your team. You must be willing to get over the potential embarrassment of asking for help if you need it. That is being a good teammate. You must also be willing to offer, even insist on help, when you see it is needed. This is only possible if you have created an environment of trust first. You accomplish that through authenticity and vulnerability. For more, read The Five Dysfunctions of a Team, by Patrick Lencioni. I have been successful in business only by the virtue of teamwork. Somehow, I understood early in my career that everything happens through people, so you must be good to people.

I have been lucky to have some great team members and many who most people thought were mediocre when I got them. But when we worked together as a high-performance team, they were very successful. After 7 years as vice-president of the General Motors business unit at Autoliv, a colleague told me that I was nothing special and had not really done anything great, since the only reason I was successful was that I had a great team, and they did all the work. In one way, they were right. My team was very good, and they did much of the work that made us successful. And it wasn't by accident that I had such good team members. One of the main ones is Sean Nayeri, who was about to be fired a few years earlier when I brought him to my team. He wasn't seen as a good performer then. But through great teamwork, he became a top performer, as did many others, and now I had the best team, and others thought it wasn't fair. But they weren't the best performers before my team, but teamwork brings out the best in people, and that is what made the team, and by extension, them so successful.

In summary, teamwork wins…in families, in sports, and in business. It is the secret. When a team is failing in sports, the first thing people talk about is the poisoned atmosphere in the locker room and the lack of teamwork. You can have the best players, but no teamwork, and you will fail spectacularly with high visibility. The opposite is also true: when a team of average players overachieves, everyone notes the love and the chemistry in the team. That is teamwork. What teams are you on in life right now? Clearly, one is your family. But there are others at work, at school, in your sports club, and at church. Think back on your best team experience. Look at your notes. What made it great? What behaviors can you put in place to make the teams you are part of even better? Where do you need to ask for help? Or dig a little deeper? Or keep your commitments? Or offer to help someone else? Or focus on the team goal and not just what's in it for you? The best for you will be when the team succeeds.

Chapter 14:
Proximity Is Power

"You are the average of the five people you spend the most time with."

~ Jim Rohn, renowned author, motivational speaker, and entrepreneur

Who are you spending your time with? Go ahead and name the three people you spend the most time with. If there are three living with you, then name the three you spend the most time with that don't live with you. Are they friends? Coaches? Colleagues? Teachers? Now think about other ways you spend your time. How much time do you spend reading? How much time playing video games? Alone or with online friends? Watching videos? Do those people you spend the most time with help you be a better person? Do they lift you up and make you feel good about who you are? Do they inspire you to do your best and be the best 'you' you can be?

You become who you hang out with! It is one of life's greatest truths. When you hang out with people, you put your focus on them and therefore become like them. Harvard professor Dr. Nicholas A. Christakis and UCSD associate professor James H. Fowler show this in their book, *Connected: The Surprising Power of Our Social Networks and How They Shape Our Lives*. They show how our relationships affect our dating, drinking, eating, and happiness habits. For example, if we have a friend who becomes obese, we are 57% more likely to as well.

Additionally, a study of 500 school children that consisted of 250 pairs of best friends in the journal *Social Development* showed that, "children who establish and maintain relationships with high-achieving students experience gains on their report card grades." Choose your friends wisely! Hang out with people who inspire you! Choose teammates and coaches who push you to be your best. Be around people who see your potential, not just where you are, and build you up towards that potential. Have a mentor or parent who helps you do things you didn't know you could do, who helps you see past what you can see for yourself.

This applies to all forms of spending time. If you hang out only in the virtual reality world of video games, you will become more like the characters there or the people that you are hanging out with in person or online, playing the games. If you read non-fiction books, you are hanging out with those authors, and you will become more like them. I have been greatly influenced by many authors whom I had not met at the time. When I was a junior at Tennessee Tech and feeling *extremely* discouraged and down, I read many books by Og Mandino. My favorite was *A Better Way to Live.* I read the same chapter in that book every morning for many months, and I transformed. It gave me hope for the future and a blueprint of how to run that day in front of me. It gave me the strength to get out of bed some days when I really didn't want to or didn't think I could. It carried me. That is the power Og Mandino had over me—by me hanging out with him, even if only through his books.

Purposeful Living

You are influenced by the people you give your attention to. I can remember being at a Tony Robbins workshop and him asking me who I spent the most time with outside my family and if that person influenced me the most in my life. It did not match. The person outside my family who influenced me the most at that point was Gustaf Celsing, and we did not see each other very often. But when I thought about it, I realized that we did spend a lot of time on the phone, talking nearly every day. And even when we were not talking, I would think about the advice he gave me and would ask myself, "What would Gustaf do now?" So, I was "hanging out" with him the most, even if it was on the phone or in my head.

I have another friend, Lisa, whom I love to hang out with and have been friends with for over 30 years. She always talks to me about where my life is going and what gifts I have that I can't see for myself. She has been seeing me as the CEO of a big company for almost 20 years, long before I could imagine it for myself. She told me long before I made enough money to afford it that I should hire someone to remodel the inside of my house because my time was much more valuable than that. She was RIGHT! She also told me to buy wonderful diamond earrings for my wife after the birth of Sawyer, our second child, and one beautiful diamond for each child. I said, "I can't afford $3,000 for diamonds!" To which she replied, "Your wife has just given you the two biggest gifts of your life. She deserves it. Put it on your credit card! You will not notice the money in a few years, but you and Tonya will never forget the priceless gift you gave her this week!" She was right! They are still the nicest pieces of jewelry Tonya has, and that gift has added immensely to our relationship. Not in the material sense, but in what the gesture meant, and still means. Lisa inspired me, pushed me, and encouraged me to be more than I thought I could be. And because of that and her, I lived up to it.

Another such friend for me is Patrick. He is a very interesting man—fluent in several languages, has a master's degree from Stanford and a Ph.D. from École Polytechnique, and has lived in 6 countries, had two wives, and been president of a large company, as well as spent 6 months meditating in Nepal. Those all make him interesting, but they are not the main reason I like this friend. Where most people look at me and say, "Wow! You did an amazing job running that Great Wall Marathon!" or "Congratulations on being President of Autoliv China!", he looks at me and says, "I know you can do better." He is always encouraging me to grow, stretch, and try to be more, to be outside my comfort zone. He sees possibilities for me that I don't see for myself, and that helps me to see them for myself. Like Lisa, he sees the potential in me and is always encouraging me to go for it. This is the kind of friend I want to be around, one who brings out the best in me, not trying to hold me back. That is why he and I have been seeing each other a few times a year, even when we live on different continents.

This is also very clear in my running. I now hang out with runners. Many of my best friends in Asia and the US now are runners, and after many years of being a "jogger," I am also now a runner. I am a runner because I hang out with runners. It started virtually, by reading many books by Jeff Galloway and practicing what he said and then moved to running with friends and meeting new friends running and hanging out with them. And running is one place where I also get supported to be more and do more. As you know, Uncle Andy is also a very good runner. When I share with him that my goal for this half-marathon is 1:55, he says, "You can do it in 1:49. Go for it!" And I do. At that Detroit Half, I didn't get to 1:49, but I did reach 1:51 and got 1:46 later in Nashville.

It works the other way as well. If you hang out with people who do bad things, you will also start to do bad things. If you hang out with people who see you as less than you are, you will become less than you are capable of being. For example, my best friend in high school was at least as smart as me, much better at football, had a cool car, was very popular, and had many girlfriends. At first, this seems to be the kind of guy I should hang out with and be like. And we did have a very good friendship. But there were two really destructive things that he did: the first was smoking a lot of pot, and the second was not doing his schoolwork. He would skip school, and even when he was there, he would not pay any attention to what was going on in class. I used to tell him, "I understand that you cut school to play golf or go hiking with a girl, but if you are in the classroom, you might as well pay attention. You are not golfing or hiking, you are here anyway, and you can't do anything else, so you have nothing to lose by paying attention." He still wouldn't. So even though he was smarter than me, he almost didn't graduate since he gave no attention and effort to his schooling. He also started hanging out with those who did a lot of harder drugs and not much else. We were scheduled to be roommates in college, and I was looking forward to that as I thought the change of environment and hanging out with college students would do him good. But he didn't show up on the first day of school. I then had to make a choice: am I going to keep hanging out with him and become like that, or am I going to stop hanging out with him and continue my education, my path? I made the difficult choice and stopped hanging out with him.

I have followed up with his parents a few times to see how he was doing and found out he got a job cutting up chickens, married a girl, had some kids, got divorced, lost his job, and was living on the streets at one point. This is not what I want to become. I am glad I made the choice to hang out with other people.

Summary:

Proximity is power! There are all kinds of ways to be in proximity to others, whether physical, social media, video games, books, talking on the phone, or texting. Proximity is whoever you have with you in your head, whoever you give your attention to. Look back at the list you made at the beginning of the chapter. Do the people you give the most attention to make you want to be better? Do they bring out the best in you? Do you feel energized and optimistic when you are with them? If so, keep it up. If not, who do you know that inspires you? Write down three, whether they are local friends or content creators on YouTube, and see how you can spend more time with them and less with the ones that make you feel bad. Proximity is power. Choose your friends and focus wisely.

Chapter 15:
Options Are Good

"I always say, do not make plans, make options."

~ Jennifer Aniston, one of the world's highest-paid
actresses

Alex, do you remember when you did not do your "solving simultaneous equations" homework and lied to Mom about doing it? Then, when you and I were working on it that night, you started by saying it was not possible and too hard, and you couldn't do it, and it wasn't worth it anyway. Do you remember? I do. You told me that even your tutor, Rachel, couldn't figure it out, so it wasn't possible. And do you remember what I told you? That your dad is pretty good at math, even better than Rachel, and that I thought we could figure it out. You felt it wasn't important. But it is important because it gives you options. It gives you choices. Doing well at whatever you are doing brings more options to you: to continue doing that or to do something else. This is true in all areas of life. And the compounding effect is greatest with respect to education. If you do well in school, many doors open to you, and you get to choose which one you want to walk through. There are many options. Do I want to go to college? Would I like to go to this college or that one? What do I want to study: premed, engineering, art, or business? Should I accept this scholarship or that one? Should I go for a semester abroad or stay home? For each little bit worse you do in school, for each time you give up or feel it is not worth it, you lose some of those options. You choose, by not applying yourself and doing your best, to give up some of your options. You forfeit your votes to someone else. First, it is just fewer scholarships, then fewer choices of universities, then fewer options for majors. Then, only community colleges, and finally, no college at all. Or even worse, you give up so much that you don't even graduate from high school. WOW! Then you have severely limited your options! What kind of job can you get when you don't graduate from high school? McDonalds? Walmart, maybe? Maybe a janitor or sanitation worker. Don't get me wrong, those are all honorable things that need to be done by someone, and if it is your calling, please pursue it. But out of choice, not because you gave away all our choices. This track also seriously limits your financial options in life. You will never fly anywhere, or stay in a nice hotel, or buy nice clothes, or a home. You simply can't do that on minimum wage.

On the flip side, if you do your best in school and life. If you push outside your comfort zone. If you do as Johann von Goethe says, and fully commit yourself, then providence moves also, and you will have options that you could never imagine. When I was a young boy growing up on the farm or even a high school student in the small town of Monterey, TN, I would never have guessed I would eventually live in Europe, let alone China! If you had told me that I would be president of a $1.5B company in China and that I would speak two languages, have two million-dollar homes, and have traveled all over the world, I would have said you were crazy. But I have. How has that happened? I have committed myself and done my best every step of the way, which has brought me choices. Albeit, with some great coaching and mentoring, I have made more good choices than bad ones and kept doing my best, and the doors kept opening, and more options became available. Options are good. Whether you want to be a painter like Picasso, a teacher, a veterinarian, an author, or a businesswoman (or all the above), the way to do it is to have the choice to make for yourself at each step of the journey. Keep doing your best, and you will have those choices. Do less than your best, and you will find your choices are made for you, and you may not like the result.

Summary:

Do your best in every situation. If the class is required, apply yourself even if you don't like it. When you are playing sports, go for it! See what you can do. When you do your best, you will have no regrets, and more options will be open to you. If you do just what is easy or what you feel like, it will reduce the options you have until at some point where you don't want any of them. Clearly, you won't take all the options you have but having them is good. Life is more interesting and more fun. Options are good.

Chapter 16:
The Power of Thought

"Whether you think you can or you can't, you are right."

~ *Henry Ford, founder of Ford Motor Company*

My son Alex reminded me how true this was when we were working on his high school math homework online. He was tired and, in a hurry, so he guessed a few answers instead of figuring them out. Naturally, he got them wrong and then got so stressed, saying again and again, "I just can't do it! I CAN'T DO IT! I CAN'T DO IT!" He was right. With that mindset, being dysregulated and hyperventilating, he couldn't do it and stomped off in a huff. And the problems were tricky, needing a few clear steps to get to the correct answer. It would take slowing down, taking a deep breath or two, writing down the steps to do it, but he could do it...if he thought he could. Each of these steps could have started with thinking to yourself, "Ok, I can do this! They would not have given it to me if I couldn't do it. I have done many like this already. I can do it! I just need to figure it out. If he had had that conversation in his head, I know he would have completed it without much time or effort at that point. Either way, you are right, but you get to choose what you think and what you say to yourself. That is what he did after taking some time to cool off; he came back with the mindset that he could do it, and he did.

So, let me ask you, what is your primary voice inside your head? When you are confronted with a challenge, what is your default mode? Do you tend to say to yourself, "I can't

107

do it"? Do you come up with all those reasons that we all have about why you can't do it? You know the list. I just can't. I am not smart enough. It is too hard. I am too young (or old). I don't know enough. My teachers didn't teach me. I don't know how. I am tired. I don't have enough money. It's too much of a risk. I don't have the energy. I am bored. I am distracted. I don't feel well. The list can go on forever. Or does the voice in your head have the other dialogue? The one that says, "I don't see how right now, but I will figure it out. I am good at challenges. I will find a way. When there's a will, there's a way." If you had to choose one voice to focus on, which one is more like you? How is it working out for you? Take some time to reflect on it here before continuing. Please use the prompt below and write it down here five times to see what comes up.

When confronted with a challenge, I…

1. _____

2. _____

3. _____

4. _____

5. _____

What comes up for you? Do you tell yourself you can do it, or you can't? Or is it a mix of both?

If you start thinking you can do it, and overcome it, you will be right. The next question becomes, "How can I do this?" not "Can I do this?" And that question is infinitely more powerful. It is an opening. It finds solutions. As soon as you ask how you will be on the path to finding the way to do it. And you, with some perseverance and providence (it takes both), you will figure it out, and you will do it.

Reflecting on my own life, I see countless examples. Two that jump to mind right now are the three-day, 100 km ultramarathon in the mountains of Yunnan Province, China, and when I became a global VP of a $6B company at age 31.

When a friend mentioned to me that he was doing a 100-kilometer running stage trail race, I said, "I could never do that." And at that point, I was right, because of my mindset. He kept encouraging me, and I kept running. About a year later, I saw an ad for such a race in a beautiful place that also had a 60 km version. That created a thought, "I could do a 3-day 60 km trail race." With that thought, I started training on trails. I registered for the race and then did the Hong Zhou and Nanjing Mountain as training. I kept running and getting in better shape. Day one of the race was in Lijiang, China, and the race director was explaining the day ahead and showing us the route for the 60 km race, which was through this town, and that one, and the 100 km was up on that ridge and across the mountains and back. I didn't come all this way to run through towns! I wanted to see the mountains. Motivated by that, I asked if I could change to the 100 km. After grilling me about my training, the race director agreed, and I was off on my first 100 km stage trail race, which I had thought was impossible only a year before.

Chapter 16: The Power of Thought

At the end of the first day and first marathon, I was completely spent, and it was clear that I could not continue and finish the 100 km, and that I should change back to the 60 km course. If I had acted on that thought, I would have been right. Luckily, my friend Andrew had a different opinion. He said, "Wait until the morning and see how you feel. If you can take a step, then maybe you can take two or 40,000." I took that advice and started to think, "Maybe I can." When I woke up the next morning, my legs hurt so much that I almost fell down trying to get out of bed, and I started to doubt again. But then I realized, even with the pain, I could walk and even go down the stairs holding onto the railing. I started to think, "Maybe I can." In fact, I feel good enough to give it a try, and if I can't, then I can always turn back. The start was brutally painful as with each step, my legs ached, but they ached a little less as I went. Within an hour of running, my legs felt good, and the voice was stronger. "I can do this!" A smile came back to my face, and I finished 3rd in my age group in my first 100 km mountain ultramarathon! It all started with pushing out the thought that I couldn't do it and replacing it with the thought, "I can do this!"

In the second story, I was living and working for Autoliv, a large, global automotive safety parts supplier, in southern Germany. On my 31st birthday, I got a call from my two bosses, tough old German Geschäftsführer Rolf Henke and hard-driving but friendly Swedish president Lars-Gunnar Skötte. I answered the phone in the car on my way home, and they started singing Happy Birthday to me. I was shocked! No-nonsense Rolf singing me happy birthday?!

Needless to say, nothing like this had ever happened to me before, and I really enjoyed it. I was a little suspicious, too. Then the other shoe dropped. "We need you to take a big job back in the US," Lars-Gunnar started. "It is a really important job, and you will really like it."

"I can't!" I replied. "I have not finished my work here. I have only been here two of my planned three years, and I haven't even launched our first new project yet. And I don't want to move back to Detroit. My wife doesn't like it there."

"You are really capable, and the company wants you to take this job, Art," Rolf spoke up next.

"I need to know what it is, and I need to finish my work here, and then we can talk," I said. To which they promised to call me back later.

Later, the Global Human Resources VP called and told me the job they were offering me was the Global VP of the General Motor Business Unit and they would like me to start within the next few months. I thought immediately, "I can't do that! I don't know how. It is too big. I can't manage a bunch of people who used to be higher than me in the company. I don't want to live in Detroit. I can't interact with people that high up in GM. I can't." And I told the HR VP as much.

At that point, I said I could not, and therefore I could not. I was right about not being able to do it because I said no before I even got started. Thankfully, a few months later, the CEO called and explained that he was a very experienced businessman, and he knew that I could do it. Furthermore, I should trust his judgment more than my own in this case. I still listed my concerns about taking it, but was already thinking, "Maybe I can do this. If I could change this and have that help, then maybe I can do it." I talked to my mentor, Gustaf Celsing, and he also felt I was the right person for the job and that I could do it, and he promised to guide me. I reflected on it for a couple of months and started thinking, maybe he did know better than me, and with my mentor's help, I could do it. I told the CEO that I would consider it and would simply do my best, and the results would be on him, as he is the one who thinks I am the right one for the job. He agreed, which took a lot of pressure off. I took it. It was not easy. I struggled. And the whole time, I was thinking that I could do this. The CEO and my mentor must know better than me, and if they think I can do it, then I can do it. Not only did I do it, but to such a high level that we tripled the business, received a top industry award, and were promoted to president of the company's fastest-growing division. It was not easy, and when I thought I couldn't, I was right, and when I thought I could, I was right!

Summary and Actions:

That is how it works. We all have the choice of what to think, and whichever way we choose to think reflects directly in the results. Thinking you can't ends the process, ensuring that you can't do it. Thinking you can opens up your mind from "Can I do it?" to "How can I do it?" This shift starts you down the path to making it happen. If you hold that mindset, you have a much greater chance of success. Think of it like this: making even a small change in how you approach things can start a chain reaction of positive outcomes. It's a bit like starting with a single step on a long hike; that first step is part of what gets you to the end. By deciding to view things differently or tweaking how you act day by day, you're setting off a ripple effect. This doesn't just change you; it can also inspire those around you to think or act differently.

This idea is similar to something called the butterfly effect in chaos theory. It's a fancy way of saying that small actions can have big consequences. Just like a butterfly flapping its wings might eventually lead to a storm far away, a small shift in your attitude or behavior can lead to major changes in your life. It shows how connected things are and how a little change now can end up making a big difference later.

What is something you want to do, but think you can't? Write down three things here.

I want to do but think I can't....

1. _____

2. _____

3. _____

Now, what if you could do them? Just pretend for a minute that you could do them. Or what do you need to do to start to believe you could do them? What would be the first step? Write it down here.

Chapter 16: The Power of Thought

The first step for each goal.

1. _____

2. _____

3. _____

Whether you think you can or think you can't, you are right.

Chapter 17:
What You Think About,
You Bring About

"I know for sure that what we dwell on is who [or what] we become."

~ *Oprah Winfrey*

This builds on what we discussed in the last chapter. Not only is it true that whether you think you can or can't, you are right, but what you think about, what you give your attention and energy to, you actually bring that about. Alex, do you remember after Easter 2015 when you were lying on the kitchen floor, complaining that you could not do anything because you had a couple of fiberglass splinters in your left hand? I do. You had been having a great day. We had just driven back from Oma and Poppy's, and you were planting flowers and jumping on the trampoline, and in between, you were shooting your bow and arrow in the backyard. You had somehow slid the bow or the arrow between the index and middle fingers of your left hand and got some fiberglass splinters in your hand. Then you were rolling around the floor crying and saying you couldn't do anything because of these splinters in your hand. You were focusing completely on this pain in your hand and thinking only about how you hate fiberglass and that you couldn't do anything because of this pain. And what you think about, you bring about. So, you were right. You couldn't do anything because that's what you were thinking about and convinced yourself of that. I tried to get you to focus on something else so you could bring that about instead. But in your tired state, that was not happening. By thinking about the pain, you were bringing it about, making it happen. Our brains are hard-wired that way. We saw an example together recently of that on Nat Geo's *Brain Games*. They had been showing how you could significantly reduce pain in your body just by looking at the part of your body that was hurting through binoculars turned around backward. This tricks your brain into thinking the hurting part, the pain, is very far away from you so you dissociate from it, making the pain reduce greatly or disappear altogether. This is thinking that the hand is too far away to be mine, so the pain must not be mine, and that thinking brings it so.

Ever since I first visited China in 2004, I thought about living there. I was intrigued. Later, in 2006, we adopted you, Kayli, and I thought even more about living there. Tonya and I even looked for a good job opportunity there that ended up being in Japan, but it did not materialize, as we had not thought about living in Japan. Then, when I started my own business, I planned to open a plant there and spend the summers there running that plant. I thought a lot about it, how you guys could learn Mandarin, and how much of an advantage that would give you in life. I kept thinking about it even as my business was failing and even as I was going to work for Autoliv again, maybe in Detroit or commuting. Then, all of a sudden, Autoliv offered me a job in China, and we all decided to take it, and we moved there. So even though I didn't get there in the way that I thought I would, I did get there because I kept thinking about it.

Sawyer, remember Shanghai and how often thinking about school was making you sick? It was awful! Stomach aches and cramps. You couldn't get off the couch. You were missing a lot of school, and we were getting really concerned about your health and whether you would progress to the next grade. Then we started to notice that it happened usually before big assignments were due. I asked you what was going on, and you said you were very afraid of doing poorly on those big assignments, whether it was a test or a major project, and if you did poorly on that, you might fail the semester. You were thinking about failing the fourth grade. You were so nervous and so focused on failing school that you were making yourself sick from the stress. And here's the interesting part, besides missing so much school for being sick, you were doing fine. There was no risk of failing. But, because of missing so much school, there was a possibility that you could have failed the grade, and that possibility was increasing every time you missed school. You were thinking about failing school, and that thinking was making you nervous and sick. And that being sick and missing school was the only way that you were going to fail school. This is a very concrete example of how what you think about is what you bring about. Once we were very clear that you were not going to fail school and that even if you did, it wouldn't really matter because we were moving back to the US, you were much healthier, and your grades started to improve, eliminating the risk of failing. It works just as well when you turn it around, you start to think about passing school and being fine in the US, even if you didn't pass. Taking that pressure off yourself and starting to think you could pass, you quit being sick and did well the rest of the year. What you thought about, you brought about.

This type of worrying is one of the best negative examples I've ever seen of "What you think about, you bring about." I love the quote from Esther Hicks, spiritual channel and best-selling author, that says, "Worrying is using your imagination to create what you don't want." I love the way Mark Twain says it. "I am an old man now who has known many troubles, most of which never happened." Worrying is thinking about what we *don't* want! What if this happens? What if that happens? And, by thinking about it, we are bringing that about. What we want to do instead is to think about what we *do* want. We want to focus on what we want to create, what we want to do, and who we want to be. All three of you kids wrote on your family goal poster one year ago that you want to have straight A's in school. Think about having straight A's. Put your attention there. Think about how good it's going to feel when your report card comes home with straight A's! Think about the rewards in life and from Mom and Dad. Think about how proud you will be with a straight-A report card. When you think about that, then you also bring that about. Then the homework won't seem so hard at night because you will be motivated by the good grades you're earning. In class, you'll be thinking about good grades and therefore paying attention instead of talking to your friend. Your focus on what you want will drive the actions that will bring that about.

When I learned to snowboard, I learned a concrete lesson about this focus. It was an icy day years ago at Bridger Bowl, MT. First, don't learn to snowboard on an icy day!

Anyway, the teacher was really clear to look where you want to go, not where you don't want to go. He said you will automatically go where you look. At the end of the day, I was beat up but finally got the hang of it and went up on my first blue run. On the way down, there was a big tree right in the middle, and I started to freak out, looking right at it and feeling like I was going to crash into it. I was headed right for it and picked up speed. Then I heard the voice of my teacher, "Look where you want to go!" It was very hard, but I forced myself to turn my head and look at the open space where I wanted to go. That was all it took. My snowboard seemed to turn all by itself, and I safely cleared the tree and stopped to collect myself. When I was looking at the tree, no matter how hard I tried to go somewhere else, I was on a collision course with it. As soon as I put my attention somewhere else, I went there.

As you are older now, I want to share another process that demonstrates this so well. It is called the DRL, or day in the remarkable life. Debbie Millman, one of the most successful and famous graphic designers in the world, was asked to do this process in her design class by a teacher who was a world-renowned designer at the time. This process is simply to start writing an essay titled A Day in the Remarkable Life of Your Name. You put yourself 10 years in the future, if a student, and 5 years if an adult, and put that date on it. Then imagine every little detail of your day exactly how you would want it to be at that time. The key is to have every detail and to keep writing in a stream of consciousness for at least 30 minutes. The one I wrote on August 20, 2021, starts like this. "I woke this morning with

119

a broad, relaxed smile. It is still dark outside at 5 AM, and I ease out of the 800-count cotton sheets in my temperature-regulated bed and out the door onto the deck with a great view where I can see it just lightening in the East." I wrote about interactions with the key people in my life: family, friends, and professional colleagues. I cover adventure, love, connection, work, eating, play, and my spiritual processes, who I am within each situation, how our interactions are, and how I am feeling. Once it is written, go back and read it every 3-6 months and see how it magically takes form. It is a great tool to focus your thinking on what you want to create.

Summary and Actions:

In summary, where our attention goes, energy flows, and that creates our life. What we think about we bring about. Make sure you are paying attention to where you want to go, not where you don't want to go, which is worrying. Set the book down now and write your DRL. Come back when it is done. Did you write your DRL? If not, set down this book and do that. Good, what came up for you? How do you feel reading it? Set a reminder in your phone or calendar to read it every three months going forward. When you catch yourself worrying, remind yourself that most of the things you worry about will never happen, and put your attention back on what you want and see how that comes to fruition.

Remember, refining your focus is like steering a ship; the smallest turn of the wheel can change your course. Keep your thoughts aligned with your goals and watch as your journey unfolds in the direction of your dreams.

Purposeful Living

Chapter 18:
Your Actions Matter

"Great things are done by a series of small things brought together."

~ *Vincent Van Gogh*

Have you ever thought, "Awe, if I do this, it won't make any difference" when thinking about some small transgression or questionable behavior? Did you ever drop a small piece of litter on the ground, thinking this little piece of trash won't make any difference? Have you taken a small souvenir from a historical tourist site, telling yourself that just taking this one small piece of ruins won't damage it?

Alex, when you were 14 and we were skiing in Gatlinburg, you kept hitting the ski lift poles with your ski poles as we went by. When I asked you why, you said, "It doesn't hurt anything, so why not?" And in a way, you are right. The pole is already rusty in that area because so many other people have hit it, and your one hit won't make any noticeable difference by itself. But the pole was very rusty where it had been hit thousands of times by thousands of people, and now there was a section 3-4 feet high that was very rusty. You did not do that by yourself, but everyone else, with the same justification that you made, has really damaged the pole. Now it will have to be sanded and repainted, when it would have lasted many more years if you and others had not had that behavior. Here is the kicker. There is no escaping it. Now your behavior, together with everyone else's, drives higher costs for the ski resort, and we all pay for that in the higher lift ticket prices.

It is the same way with littering. As you told me in China, "Daddy, it doesn't make any difference since there is so much litter on the ground already." But if everyone thinks and behaves that way, it will all be disgusting to look at. And that is the price we all pay. We all get to live in a junk pile! On the flip side, your one action can make a big difference. If you don't litter, you will feel better about yourself, and if everyone doesn't, the world will be a much better place. Taken one step further, if you pick up some litter, you can bring your street back from being a junk pile.

Remember how much we hated the litter on the street between our house and the front of your school in Shanghai? So, we behaved in a way that if everyone did the same, the world would be a much nicer place. We went out on Tomb Sweeping Day in 2012 and picked up 6 trash bags of litter along that street. Remember how good that felt? I think you, Alex, won a contest for who could fill up the most bags. Do you remember what happened next? The headmaster was horrified that one of his customers, a "gentleman" like himself, was out picking up litter. He came and talked to me about it, and he was so shocked and apologized so much. He never let litter build up there again. He got his guards to stop littering (They were one of the biggest contributors) and had his Ayi clean it on a regular basis. Our world was a much better place with clean streets to walk on to school each morning. And every other family that went to school there had a much better experience, too, which benefits them and the school. Everyone wins. The cumulative effect of all these small actions will make your community and the world a better place or a worse place. Choose to do the actions that will make it better for all, even if it is a very small difference.

There is another effect of these small, good or kind actions. Let me recount the starfish story. A boy came down to the beach much as he did many mornings, but this morning the beach was covered with starfish. Knowing they would die if they didn't get back in the water and feeling compassion, he started picking one after another and putting them back in the ocean. A man asked him what he was doing. He said, 'I am putting starfish back in the water.' The man said he was foolish. There were thousands of starfish on the beach, and there was no way he could save them all. It wouldn't make any difference. The boy put another one back in the ocean and said it made a difference to that one. It saved one's life. Yes, it was not possible for him to save them all, but it matters to that one. It is the same in life. You likely can't solve homelessness by giving a coat to the man under the bridge or serving meals at your church as part of Room in the Inn, which takes in the homeless for a night, but it will make a big difference to that person, to those people you helped. The smile you give to a stranger will make a difference to them. The kindness you give to your server will make a difference to them. And these small kindnesses also make a difference to you. You will also feel good about what you did to make things a little better, instead of feeling bad about the big problem out there you cannot solve.

Your actions *do* matter! Any time you think they don't, ask yourself, "What would happen if everyone did this?" Then take the action that would make the world a better place if everyone did what you are about to do! Ask yourself if it will make a difference to the one person or thing you are improving or degrading. Do the thing that makes that one life better, that one street cleaner, that one space kinder. You will feel better, and the world, or at least that one person or community, will thank you!

Chapter 19:
Challenges Bring Us to Life

"Comfort is like a sedative that numbs us to the richness and depth of life."

- Michael Easter, Author of The Comfort Crisis

Stop and reflect. In the last month, when did you feel the most alive? When did you feel your entire body vibrating at high frequency? Have you come up with something yet? If not, go back in time until you find one. I have mine. It was last Thursday when I was standing on the ridge, I had just hiked up 4 feet of snow at the top of the Hidalgo run in Toas. When I dropped off the cornice and hit the powder on that incredibly steep run, I was totally ALIVE! It is a big challenge and very hard and scary, and that is what brings me alive! What is yours? It could also be standing up in front of your boss and his team to give the performance update or the sales pitch you have been working on for the last month, teaching your favorite class, or caring for your child. What is it for you? I bet it is something that is also challenging and scary.

Sawyer, how did you feel when you jumped from the top of the pole and caught the trapeze when we were doing the ropes course? Or when you got 100% on your Victorian Project presentation at school? Alex, what about when you nailed the backflip on the trampoline for the first time? Kayli, when you finally got the perfect gymnastics floor routine? Or hip over? How about when you finally got to that next level on a video game that has been "impossible" until now? You feel great! That is the funny thing about life. It is not comfort, but challenges, doing hard things, and difficulty, that make us feel good.

When I was running my second Shanghai Marathon, it was cold, windy, and rainy, with bad air quality. It was very difficult! At mile 17, I was pushing myself hard to still finish in under 4 hours. I was at the point where I could break out crying or laughing at any moment, which happens in every marathon. I was thinking to myself, "This is really, really hard! But it is still good! How can it be both hard and good?" I asked myself, "Why is it that when I have a hard day at work, I label it bad, but I can be having a VERY hard day in the race and still call it good?" It is a paradigm. It is simply the way I have programmed myself to think about these things. Somewhere along the way, I learned that hard days were bad days...at school, at work...at a very young age. And that has stuck with me all these years, until I saw through running that I can do things that are mind-bogglingly hard, and they really suck at the time, but I feel great at the finish. During the race, I am yelling and cursing myself. It is that difficult, and yet, in the end, I feel so good. I am beaming, ecstatic, telling everyone I know, "You have to come do this. It is AWESOME!" It has become abundantly clear to me that we are happy when we overcome challenges, when we do something that is beyond what we think we could do. We experience joy when we push past our limits, when we do something that is very challenging, scary, or uncomfortable. That is the only way to discover this "bigger" us. And discovering that "bigger" us is always a joy.

Right after the realization during the Shanghai marathon, I stopped calling hard days at work 'bad days,' just hard days. And when someone at work started saying, "But Boss, that is so hard!" I would say "Yes, it is! That is why I have given it to you. You can do it! And when you do, you will feel great!" It even became a core value at work: "We do hard things!" You may have heard me say that to you as well, and I will continue to do so. When you say, "Daddy, this is so hard!" I say, "That's right, Sweetie, it is!" And I will say it with a big smile and genuine excitement, knowing that you will feel so good when you get it done!

Physical challenges are the most obvious ones, and that is why there is an explosion of participants in Tough Mudders, Spartans, Ultra Marathons, and Iron Man Triathlons. These are all people looking to challenge themselves, to see what they are made of. But you can do it in other areas too, academically, work, and creativity. In each of these areas, you can pick a goal that calls to you but is also very difficult, way outside your comfort zone. If you choose to go for it, there will be times in the middle that suck where you want to quit, and it doesn't seem worth it. But if you stick with it and get to the finish, you will feel great. That I promise.

Comfort is also good in moderation. We all need rest and relaxation. And having a comfortable space where we feel safe and nurtured is necessary. And it is a retreat. It is the place to come back to when you have done something really challenging. However, if we spend all our time in our comfort zone, we will be depressed. The only growth we have in our comfort zone is the recovery of doing something that really stretches us. And we are only happy when we are growing. Yes, spend some time in comfort, but don't make it your focus. Make sure you also spend plenty of time outside your comfort zone. How do you do that? Practice! Do small things that are uncomfortable, like taking a cold shower for 30 or 60 seconds at the end of your shower, apologizing for a mistake when you don't feel like it, pushing yourself a little harder when your lungs or legs are already on fire, or volunteering for the new task at work that is a little scary. When you practice in these small ways, you are building the muscle to be able to take on the bigger challenges that excite and scare you, like doing a marathon, taking that job overseas, getting married, or starting that business.

It is a good thing that challenges make us feel alive because life is full of them. Life is a challenge or a struggle, and if you choose your struggles, it is also an amazing journey. I have tried to find a kinder, gentler way of putting it, but life is a struggle. And that is good. There are two kinds of struggle, or some people and religions call it suffering. The first one is one that chooses you. This is the one that looks like it happens to you. It can be the struggle to recover from an addiction to drugs or alcohol. It can be the struggle to lose weight. It can be a struggle to overcome an illness or injury. You can still grow in spirit and learn a lot from this type of struggle. But usually, the best you can do is to get back to where you were before that struggle. It is a struggle that brings you back up to the level you already were in life. It returns you to your former state of sobriety, health, or weight. It is a very real struggle, and it is noble, and it gets you back to where you were once before, plus the lessons you learned along the way. I have struggled with my weight most of my life, and each time I take the actions and am successful in meeting my target, I am then back to the weight I was before. I am back to my target weight. It is very good and it is not net progress. I am just back to where I started, plus my learning.

My best friend in high school is a good example of this first type of struggle. He and I were very similar, except he let life choose his struggles, and I largely chose mine. He was at least as smart as I was and had more money and a nice car and was a better football player, and popular, but he was not intentional. He would not choose his struggles and direct his life. Even so, he still managed to get into the same university as me, and we planned to be roommates. But he never showed up. A couple of days later, the police came to my room looking for him. He let life choose his struggles by drinking and doing drugs as a teenager and then having to struggle with recovery to get back to level ground. He never did go to college, and I have not talked to him in years, but he was married with a couple of children, then divorced, remarried, and divorced again. He was working a minimum wage job processing chicken. Last time I talked to him, he struggled every day with how to pay the bills, how to raise kids separately from their mother, and how to stay sober. He has great suffering and struggles, but all to get back to level zero because of not choosing his struggles for himself.

I had the same experience a few years ago financially. I lost all my savings in a new business venture. I suffered more than ever before in my life. It was incredibly intense, not knowing how I was going to pay the bills and take care of my family. The self-doubt that came with it was crushing. I suffered deeply and worked very hard after many years just to get back to the same level of financial stability as I had before. I have just made it back to level 0 financially, but I learned some great lessons too.

The second type of struggle or challenge is what I call intentional suffering, or the struggle that you choose. The big difference from the first type is that the struggle you choose takes you on an amazing adventure and takes you forward. It makes your life interesting, thrilling, successful, and an inspiration to others, and it feels great! There are infinite types of struggles here. Any goal that you choose and then achieve will entail some level of suffering or struggle. When you choose to go to college, you will struggle and suffer a lot there. Learning is hard and takes time, intention, and lots of confusion. And if you stick with the struggle you have chosen, you will come out on the other side with a college degree and many more options in life. If you choose to learn a sport or musical instrument, it will entail 10,000 hours of practice to master it. That is a lot of struggling. And when you do, you have achieved something great that you have worked on for your whole life.

When I first chose to run a marathon, it was a big struggle. I had to carve out lots of time in my schedule. I created lots of aches and pains and had to ice my knees with frozen veggies after every long run. My whole body hurt like crazy, and I could barely walk for the week afterward. I was only 28! I had grown tremendously as a human being, doing something that only a very small percentage of the population had done. Suddenly, some of my other problems did not seem so big, and my whole life and my confidence in my abilities had expanded. With that confidence, I took a job in Germany. Two years later, everything, especially my knee, toe, and back, was hurting. My back was so bad that I fell on the floor and couldn't move due to back spasms, so I decided to stop running. I had several good reasons, and still, my life circle got a little smaller. I was starting to let life choose my struggles for me, and I started to gain weight again, and my stress level increased. It got to a point where I needed to do something! I was very stressed and was up to 225 lbs. again, which I felt was not healthy or attractive. I had let life choose my struggles, and now I had to act to get back to my starting point.

I started walking again, doing Tony Robbins' 15 Minutes to Fulfillment every morning. Even with only 15 minutes of walking each morning, I started feeling better and dropping some weight. Slowly, I started jogging for a few minutes in the middle of the 15-minute walk, and with the help of *Galloway's Guide to Running*, I could even run/walk several miles now without any serious pain. After letting life choose my struggles for a while, I was back to level 0. My back was still an issue, but better than when I had stopped running a few years earlier. In the summer of 2004 or 2005, I was at a personal growth workshop with my brother, Andy, and was inspired to run a marathon again. Now, I had many reasons not to, primarily since I had a bad back and "running is not good for your back," as I had been told many times by doctors. However, now I was choosing my struggle. Instead of using my bad back as an excuse not to do what I wanted, I decided that I would heal my back so well that I could run a marathon. I decided to do it to make my whole life that much better. And that is what I did. It took a long time (We will talk about persistence in a later chapter.) and many hours of running and many more hours of back exercises, and I slowly worked my way back up and did the Detroit Half Marathon in 2005 and again in 2006, and I finally did a full marathon in NYC at the end of 2007. I was back to running marathons, and my back was better than ever. I was injury-free! Long story short, running, a huge struggle that I have chosen for myself, has led to amazing relationships, fun, and adventures in my life. It is what keeps me at peace and happy on a daily basis when work is super stressful. It is how I made many great friends from Shanghai to Tennessee, and I have been on the most amazing adventures of my life, running two 100-kilometer, three-day ultra-marathons in the mountains of Asia, including one with my brother Andy in the Himalayas of Nepal. That was an adventure that was beyond my imagination just a few years ago. It was also very hard and brought to me by choosing my struggle. These two expanded my belief about what is possible in my life manyfold, as well as being some of the best times of my life. Out of that chosen struggle, life has become an amazing adventure!

Conclusion and Actions:

Life is a struggle. It is a challenge. And it is in meeting that challenge, not avoiding it, that we come alive. Life begins at the edge of our comfort zone. On another amazing adventure in the summer of 2023, when all my siblings and I were backpacking unsupported in the Montana wilderness for 6 days, my brother told his seven-year-old son, "To be unburdened, you first must carry a load." That is right. We must do difficult things to feel relief when we set them down, when we complete them. That contrast is what makes life so sweet, so amazing. What have you dreamed of doing that is uncomfortable or scary? List 3 things you have thought about but seem outside your reality or capability. What are they?

Dreams that Are Scary:

1)

2)

3)

Write down one very small action you can take right now to move in that direction for all three of them. If it is to run a marathon and you haven't run at all, sign up for a 5k now. If it is to write a book, write the first sentence now. If it is to get that promotion, ask your boss what it will take to get it, or update your resume now. If it is to lose 10 lbs., choose a healthy eating plan now. Overcoming challenges brings us alive. So, life will give them to us if we don't choose them for ourselves. Embrace each challenge as an invitation to grow stronger and more resilient. By stepping forward into the unknown, you craft the narrative of your own adventure, transforming fear into a compass that guides you toward your true potential.

So, I recommend you choose! When you choose your struggle, life is an amazing adventure. Enjoy!

Chapter 20:
Progress, Not Perfection

"Perfection is the enemy of progress."

~ Winston Churchill, Supreme Commander of the Allied Forces in WWII, British Prime Minister, Author

In Workaholics Anonymous, I have learned that good enough is good and much better than nothing. I had always believed the saying "If it is worth doing, it is worth doing right!" This blocked me from getting started. If it is worth doing, it is worth doing. Striving for perfection, or doing it right, often keeps us from doing anything at all. It blocks progress of any kind. It blocks us from even getting started. The founders of Airbnb and Netflix talk about taking the minimal viable action to get started. What is the one small step we can take now to see if this idea might work? It is not grandiose, sophisticated, or anywhere near perfect. But it is progress. And look at those companies today!

I had a request for a proposal for executive coaching this week, and my first thought was to get everything perfect before I responded to this new request: to have my website polished, all partnerships in place, and a perfect billing system. That would have kept me from responding this week. Instead, I set myself a time limit, put the simple proposal together in that time, and sent it out. It is not polished, and it is the minimal viable action; it is a start. I have many examples in my home life as well. For example, I have these 3 signs from some great roads I have driven, that have been sitting in my garage for 4 years! I have told myself every time I pass them, 1-3 times per day, that I will put them up on the wall as intended when I bought them. Why didn't I do so for 4 years? I needed it done right, to have the garage painted first and have the signs laid out precisely. One day, when I was walking past them, I thought, "Progress, not perfection," and right then, I got some double-sided tape and stuck them on the wall in about 5 minutes. They look great! I have been enjoying them ever since. And the garage still isn't painted. ☺ Progress is much more important than perfection. If we waited for a perfect relationship to start, we would never be in a relationship. If we decided at 1 year old, we wouldn't walk until we could do it perfectly, and we would still be crawling. Forget that old saying, "If it is worth doing, it is worth doing right," and replace it with "progress, not perfection."

In the last couple of years, I have done many things in a way that I used to think was half-assed, but it is much better to have done good enough than not at all. We miss out on so much of life waiting for it to be perfect before we start. I encourage you to do whatever has been sitting out there, calling you to do it. What is the minimal viable action step you can do to get started on it, without being perfect, to start enjoying it? Do it! Now!

Chapter 21:
Persistence Pays

"Nothing in this world can take the place of persistence. Nothing is more common than unsuccessful men with talent."

~ *Calvin Coolidge, 30th President of the United States*

As we think back on this book, you have learned that you are worthy and loved. You have a path to finding your purpose, your grand adventure, by tuning into your Inner Voice, to God. You have learned the importance of your thoughts and your actions, and how to interact well with people. You have learned how to get started with progress, not perfection, in the last chapter. Finally, you must stick with it. Finding your passion is not enough. Have you ever heard the quote "You can do anything you set your mind to"? It is only partially true. You must set your mind to anything you want to do, and setting your mind to it is not enough. You must also set your time and energy to it. You must continue to give it your time and energy until you achieve it. As the saying goes, "Pray as it depends on God, AND then work like it depends on you!" Both are equally important. You must put in the time and energy to be successful, to achieve any goal. When you have your purpose, when you are on your path, you must persist. So many people fail to share their gifts because they stop. They quit, and it could be just inches before the breakthrough. Persevere! It can be really slow and really hard but keep going. We know that doing difficult things brings us to life, so we must persist even when it is difficult.

At about 22 miles into the Great Wall Marathon, it was really hot, around 90 degrees Fahrenheit, and I was so tired that I had a water bottle in each hand and was bear-crawling up the 1,500 steps toward that end. I was close to the top of the wall, and then it was just an "easy" 3-mile jog down a paved road to the finish. There were many people who had given up and were going back down the steps. I tried to tell them it was actually easier to finish than to go back to the previous aid station and that if they just went really slow and rested enough, they could finish. I even stopped and rested with some of them, and then I started back up as they started back down. It was hard, and persisting through the difficulty is what allowed me the joy of finishing, the joy of hitting the goal.

Most worthwhile endeavors are harder than we think in the beginning and take longer to complete. This is OK, it is part of the plan because if we had really known how hard they were, we may not have started. Our job is to persist. This tenacity is the biggest driver of human success.

And, in some ways, it gets easier as you go, as well. At first, anything you do is confusing, and you are not very good at it, which can keep it from being fun. But you will get better if you are willing to be confused and you stick with it. There was a study recently showing that if you do anything for long enough, you learn to love it. I think about myself and running. I did not like it when I started in college. I felt like I *had to* do it to get my exercise. I hated it, but I did it because I felt like I had to. After many years of feeling like I had to and not really enjoying it, even through running a marathon, I started to enjoy the way it made me feel. I stopped running due to injury, and started over again, slowly working up to another marathon. Somewhere in those seven years, I started to love running, to love the running itself. Now, when I am out running, I love it. I absolutely love it! It always puts a smile on my face and deep satisfaction in my heart. I have logged many, many hours doing it. I don't know how many, but thousands of miles. Whenever I run, I feel great, which scientists will tell you is no surprise. For 80% of people, dopamine kicks in when you run. It does for me. I love to run alone in the rain with a hat on. It is like my own private sanctuary. I love to run with friends. I love the connection, the camaraderie, and the speed at which we go, since usually my friends are faster than me. I love to run alone, listening to a book or simply being present with the lovely sky and trees and hills, and creeks where I live. It is one of the true joys in life. I have spent hours doing it, and I have learned to love it tremendously.

In Malcolm Gladwell's book, *Outliers*, he shows that you will become an expert at anything you do for 10,000 hours. If you put in 8 hours a day, 5 days a week, for 5 YEARS, you will be an expert. Or if you put in 2 hours a day, 5 days a week for 20 YEARS, you will be an expert. It takes 10,000 hours to master something, to be OUTSTANDING! This will make you one of the best in the world. He has many examples, from Bill Gates being the first human on the planet having 10,000 hours of computer programming experience, to the Beatles playing on stage 8 hours a day, 7 days a week for 4 years in Hamburg before anyone knew who they were. This is what made them great! You can see this in sports as well. The best players, all the professionals, have put in tremendous hours since they were young kids, often starting before they were 3 years old. Obviously, you can learn the basics of a sport and even be good enough to enjoy playing it for much less than 10,000 hours. You remember playing football, doing gymnastics, or learning a musical instrument. You guys had fun at that after only a season or two, putting in only a couple of hours a day. And that is great for a hobby, for fun. It will not make you professional or the best in the world.

To put in those kinds of hours to be a pro or one of the best in the world takes tremendous energy and persistence, and you will only do that if you are passionate about what you are doing and if you love it! That is why you must find something that you LOVE that you are really passionate about in order to have the energy and stamina to put in 10,000 hours.

It is much easier to put in the hours if what you are doing is a strength. In *Play to Your Strengths*, Marcus Buckingham defines strength as something that strengthens you by doing it. It is something that you love to do so much that doing it actually gives you energy instead of tiring you out! You are in the zone and can do it for very long periods without a break, and you are more excited, more energized, and feel better after having done it than you were before you started. Your strengths actually ***strengthen*** you. I like this definition of strength. When you find this strength, this passion that you love and energizes you, you will be able to put in the hours that it takes to become great at it and be able to help many people, and therefore also receive enough value to make a good living doing it as well. And the rewards come at the end. Just like compound interest, the rewards grow more rapidly the longer you stick with it. I made more in my 27th year in my career than I did in the first 15 years combined. The satisfaction of the marathon comes after hitting the wall at mile 17 and pushing through to the finish.

I am great at connecting with people and leading. And how many hours do I have to do that? Wow! I started early in my childhood, being the peacemaker in the family and learning how to connect so both parties could hear each other. Then, starting after my freshman year in college, I did a transformational personal growth workshop, every 2-3 months for 10 years. Each workshop was about 40 hours, and there were many hours in between where I was connecting with people, telling them about the workshop and its principles. That is 2,000 hours just in the workshops. Once I started work, I was leading teams by age 23 and managing a department by age 26. Full-time, 50 - 60 hours per week, and continued this for 20 years. That is 50,000 hours! I also did engineer work, financial analysis, emails, etc., so maybe I was connecting with or leading people 1/2 of that time, but it is still 25,000 hours. So yes, I have gotten very, very good at leading. I love it. I love connecting with and leading people, seeing them grow at work, at home, in their lives, as a human being, and as a whole. I love sharing ideas that inspire them to be more than they thought they could be. Nothing gives me more joy! And it has powered me through all the hard times and kept me going so that I could become great at it.

Building on that connection with people, I am now hosting the Life in Transition podcast and leading transition groups, and I love doing that. I am building on the tens of thousands of hours I have spent connecting with people and leveraging that to be an outstanding podcast host who has made it a peak experience for my guests and transformational for our listeners. And I know it will take some time, likely many years, to be great at this. I am willing to persist.

Conclusions and Actions:

Research shows that setting small, achievable goals makes the journey towards big dreams more manageable and rewarding, helping maintain motivation and focus. When you are on the right track, don't quit, don't stop. Persist! Don't think about the whole journey, business, or the end game; just take the next step. If you have it in you for one more step, take it. Then take the next one and the next. We get discouraged climbing the mountain if we are always stopping to see how far it is to the top. But if we just keep putting one foot in front of the other, it will surprise us how far we have come when we look back. Keep going. Whether it is the last class to finish your degree or the last 1,500 steps to climb to finish the Great Wall Marathon, persist. If you have it in you to take one more step, do it. The rewards are worth it. In your journey, cherish each step as progress, not just a means to an end. This mindset transforms even the smallest actions into significant milestones, fueling your perseverance and illuminating your path with purpose and passion.

Conclusion

Thank you for taking the time to read this book and hanging out with me. I hope it has and can help you find your voice, to know that you are worthy and a beloved child of God. When you find that connection to God, to your inner and highest self, that will help you find your calling, your purpose, your inspiration, your grand adventure. And that is the main job and joy in life, to find that which really lights us up, that pulls us out of bed each morning. If you get nothing else from this book, please know that you are worthy and loved, and the greatest joy comes from living your grand adventure. After that, the rest are tools that I have found helpful for my journey that I wish I had learned earlier in my life. I would have suffered much less. Hopefully, some of them resonate with you. Apply those to your life now. Look back at the action plans and notes you have made, and make sure you are doing the ones that will bring you the most value. Leave the rest, at least for now. It is much better to take one action thoroughly that really makes a difference than to start many and drop them all. In addition, if you are on your path, living your grand adventure, you will find tools and support along the way. Keep coming back here if it is helpful. Wake up each day saying "Yes!" to your grand adventure. Do whatever it takes to keep your light shining, and you will help everyone around you, including me, keep our lights shining as well. Thank you!

Appendix

Suggested Books to Read

<u>For Those Coming of Age</u>

Man's Search for Meaning, by Viktor Frankl

The Anatomy of Peace, by the Arbinger Institute

Seven Habits of Highly Effective People, by Stephen Covey

Courage Is Calling, by Ryan Holiday

How to Win Friends and Influence People, by Dale Carnegie

<u>For Parents and Caregivers</u>

The Anatomy of Peace, by the Arbinger Institute

Bonds That Make Us Free, by C. Terry Warren

Beyond Consequences, Logic, and Control, by Heather T. Forbes and B. Bryan Post

The Boy that Was Raised Like a Dog, by Bruce D. Perry and Maia Szalavitz

Hold on to Your Kids, by Gordon Neufeld and Gabor Maté

www.ingramcontent.com/pod-product-compliance
Lightning Source LLC
Chambersburg PA
CBHW051204120626
46547CB00013B/1198